FROM PEKING TO PERTH

Published by *Artlook Books*.
P.O. Box 8268, Stirling Street, Perth, Western Australia.

Copyright © Alice Briggs, 1984,

Typesetting, layout and design by *Artlook*.

Printed in Singapore.
By Singapore National Printers (Pte) Ltd.

National Library of Australia
Cataloguing in Publication data
Peking to Perth
ISBN   0   86445   049   4

Distributed in Australia and Overseas by the Publisher.

FROM
PEKING
TO
PERTH

Alice Briggs

THIS IS AN
Artbook
PUBLICATION

Foreword

It was a pleasure to pen a foreword to this deeply felt yet modest book. As the author notes, my introduction to her came about as a result of a set of curious chances scarcely less remarkable than those which are recounted in another celebrated Japanese drama — The Mikado. But war does these things.

On the evening of February 15, 1942 the incessant roar of the closing hours of Singapore died away and all was still. Bewildered troops, of whom I was one, having been ordered to throw down their arms, found themselves face to face with a future quite beyond their imagination. Even when to their surprise, it was learnt that they were destined to live — for a time at least — and not to die at the hands of the all-conquering Japanese, most of us turned to the past which alone seemed to have some meaning; the future had no meaning at all. What we all made of this situation, whether we happened to be defeated troops in an alien land or dejected civilians in a country which had once been their own, was for most of us the greatest single decision in our lives.

For many years little was written about these incredible days. It is only now, 40 years on, that details of the story are starting to find their way into print. Yet it would have been otherwise had a far sighted decision of Sir Frederick Gallaghan, the senior Australian officer in command of all that remained of the 8th Aust. Div. after over 3½ years in captivity in Changi, been carried out.

He had wisely concluded that, as the first Australian soldiers to surrender to an Asiatic power, an attempt should be made to gather from the troops under his command contemporary accounts of their experiences as prisoners of the Japanese. Whether ultimately our destiny was to live or to die, he believed that a collection of papers of some literary merit, written on the spot, dealing with the day-to-day aspects of our imprisonment would be a significant contribution to history. There was no shortage of gifted writers in Changi — some of whom have since become internationally known —; we had paper because we had learnt how to make it and we had learnt to improvise materials for writing. A number of writers were selected and they willingly went to work. The task of supervising, editing and collating all this material was alloted to me. As a result, when the atom bomb miraculously came to our rescue, I had in my possession a series of unique manuscripts dealing intimately with almost every aspect of prison life. These I carried with me by safe hand to Sydney and without delay delivered to the War Memorial Museum in Canberra. Alas, nothing came of it. The trustees decided, largely on the advice of the Prime Minister of the day, that publication be withheld. Some of the material was considered to be too harrowing for the public at large and particularly so for the devastated relatives of the thousands who died in captivity. But time, the healer, and new generations of Australians for whom the Japanese war is but an incident in our past, has stimulated a growing interest in the tragic consequences of the war against Japan.

In this book Mrs. Briggs now adds another chapter to the story. In addition to her frank and straightforward account of life as a Japanese internee, she also gives us a bonus in the form of an account of life in Peking at the turn of the century during the reign of the last Empress of China. It is as fascinating as it is unknown to most of us.

How each of us re-acted to the overwhelming experiences of imprisonment in barbaric conditions was to some extent a mirror held to his own temperament. But the essential fairness, truthfulness and compassion of Mrs. Briggs' account tells us as much about herself as about the events she describes. In this book she has made a worthy addition to the sum total of our knowledge and experience.

Sir David Griffin C.B.E., Ll.B.
Sydney, July 1984

Contents

Chapter 1
Peking 1903 15

Chapter 2
School Days and Marriage 34

Chapter 3
China 1933 - 1937 55

Chapter 4
Home Leave 82

Chapter 5
Sad Days in Hong Kong 93

Chapter 6
Internment — Survival — Release 107

Chapter 7
Homeward Bound 134

Appendix I 149

Appendix II 152

Acknowledgements

My first thanks must go to my husband Christopher whose moral and physical encouragement has helped me so greatly in achieving my wish to put pen to paper and for his patience and hard work in doing the rough drafts from my notes, also for his many helpful suggestions.

My grateful thanks to my nephew John Murray for photographing many relics, and to his wife Irene for typing the completed manuscript.

To Mrs. Pat Fox, one of my flatmates in Stanley Internment Camp, Hong Kong for 3½ years. She recently shared incidents from her diary and photographs of camp which have helped me greatly in re-capturing some of the events of those years.

To Mrs. Nell Labrousse (Nell Hale as she was in Camp) one of the elite Queen Alexandra Imperial Nursing Sisters who had done most of her nursing in India. Nell was a wonderful friend whom I had never met before the war. To her I owe much in so many ways — kindnesses given and companionship beyond price through those difficult days.

My thanks to Mrs. Peggy Batten (nee Pears) for information about Waddington, Lincolnshire; to the Imperial War Museum, London for the use of photographs of events in Hong Kong between 1942 - 1945; to the South China Morning Post; and to many friends who have encouraged and challenged me to continue writing and to finish my book; to my friends Henry and Olwyn Scott for their great interest and especially to Mrs. Zophia Kotkowski whose idea it was that I should write my story.

DEDICATED
to
My daughter Patricia
and
The many other civilians who suffered physical
and psychological deprivation or death
in the Japanese Internment Camps
of Hong Kong and South East Asia.

The author in 1953.

Introduction

In February 1976 the following article by David McNicoll was printed in *The Bulletin* and inspired me to add my experiences to this 'touch of human kindness'.

> "The usual concept of Japanese soldiers in charge of prisoners in World War II is not very flattering to our former enemies, in fact they are generally portrayed as pretty nasty bits of work.
>
> But the picture can be quite wrong. Take for instance Captain Jesuke Terai, one of the officers at Changi during the incarceration of Sir David Griffin in 1942.
>
> Terai was an interpreter at the jail and had been an academic in Japan before the war. When David Griffin and his fellow prisoner Leslie Greener started to organize amenities for the prisoners they found an enthusiastic ally in Terai.
>
> He assisted them in getting copies of plays to present at the Changi *theatre* and in scrounging costumes and scenery. He was an invaluable helper to the amateur thespians.
>
> In February last year Leslie Greener died in Tasmania, and somehow Terai got to hear about it in Japan nearly a year later.
>
> Last week David Griffin received a letter postmarked Hiroshima from Terai. In it Terai told of his sadness of Greener's death — a sadness which he regretted he found it impossible to express adequately in English."

Christmas Day 1941 was the day when a proud people in Hong Kong surrendered to an enemy who had bombed and shelled them day and night with a determination and cunning to win — a day that will never be forgotten by the European and Chinese people living in the Colony at that time.

In January 1942 I was interned in the Civilian Internment Camp in Hong Kong — situated in the centre of Stanley Peninsular and joined to the mainland by a narrow strip of sand — the only approach being a road running across the strip.

Stanley was the first settlement of the British, and on a lovely part of the hillside looking West over Stanley Bay was the 100-year-old cemetery. Buried there were a few soldiers, their wives and infants, who had died from malaria or disease. Thanks to the eradication of malaria in Hong Kong there was, to my knowledge, no case at the time of our internment. Now are added many more to the old graves of those first brave pioneers, the graves of those who died of atrocities, starvation, and malnutrition.

At the time of our internment this cemetery had been very neglected but with the hard work and loving care of a Hong Kong policeman it was a very different place when we left. He had tidied the old graves and planted cannas and bushes and we were grateful to him for his work over the years to make it a place of peace and memories. The path through the cemetery became well worn by the many internees who trod it while they still had the strength to walk round the camp area. I hope the policeman received some tangible recognition and that the cemetery is still cared for today in memory of those who suffered and lost their lives in Stanley.

First among the new graves that one comes to from the northern entry is the one holding three V.A.D. nurses, who were raped and killed, and one of Col. Dr. Black of the Hong Kong Volunteer Defence Corps who bravely tried so hard to stop this happening and keep the Japanese out of St. Stephen's Hall which had been turned into a hospital. He died trying to save the nurses and the wounded from the onslaught. How tragic and sad war is.

We were, of course, surrounded by barbed wire with perimeter lights at night. Later when allied air-raids started the lights were turned off and we felt very vulnerable.

Buildings on the peninsular included the new Hong Kong gaol — quarters for the European officers and their families — bachelor quarters — and quarters for the Indian warders and their families. At the extreme tip of the peninsular was the military fort. The fort and the gaol were not used by the internees for accommodation and were 'out of bounds'.

Also on the peninsular was St. Stephen's College referred to as the 'Eton' of Hong Kong — founded in 1903 by several prominent Chinese gentlemen who had been educated in England.

They sought the help of the Church Missionery Society in their venture so its education was on a Christian basis. There were several bungalows for the college staff. These bungalows normally accommodated up to five people but now had to accommodate up to 45 each, which gives an idea of how 3,580 people, men, women and children were crowded into this small area. On the 29th June 1942, 334 Americans were repatriated in exchange for Japanese in America and they sailed from Stanley for Lorenzo Marques.

For 3½ years I was to live in the Indian warders quarters (or flats) in a 10' by 10' room with two, sometimes three, people I had never met before the war — eating, trying to read, trying to sleep, trying to LIVE. Our camp-bed space was literally our 'home'.

I tell my simple story of that time in the hope that it will create a new awareness and positive approach to things past and in the future. My experiences were shared by many during the war with more able minds than mine to put pen to paper.

Many years have passed since the events I describe, and it is seldom that two witnesses will ever portray an event in exactly the same way. Thus others may have witnessed the same events described by me and not have seen them with the same eyes or with the same feelings.

I would like to quote from a great man of our present times, namely the Russian writer and Nobel Prize Winner Alexander Solzhenitsyn. He wrote:

"Perhaps everyone is fated to live through every experience himself in order to understand."

I know this to be true and I hope some of my experiences may help others to understand and piece together the 'jigsaw' of life.

There are many 'ifs' and 'buts' in life, decisions we feel we should have made differently — because of the uncertainties created by such an event as war. Did we do the right things and make the right decisions? A different decision might have meant no long separation and no internment but it might also have meant that one or all of us might not be here today.

But I would like to go back some years prior to my war experiences . . . to my very beginning in Peking — to my childhood, job, and marriage in England — my return to China as my home — the war years and finally to Perth, Western Australia, where I now live, and where I find links with the past are still unfolding. I hope you will join me in my life's journey from Peking to Perth.

The author and her mother, Peking.

Chapter 1

PEKING 1903 AND EARLY YEARS

On a hot July day in 1903 in the ancient city of Peking, during the reign of the last empress of China — the notorious Manchu Empress T'zu Tse — a sedan-chair was being carried from the British Legation Quarter to a small mission outside the Legation wall. Sitting inside the chair was a lovely young woman who was about to become my mother. Her name was Alice Helen Murray, nee Harden. She came from a family of five girls and two boys — the eldest Jessie, then Jack, Lina, Jane, Alice (my mother), Marion, and the youngest Allan. My mother was the 'beauty' of the family with fine features, brown eyes, chestnut-brown hair, an elegant 5ft 7'' slim figure, and a gentle sweet expression. She was nicknamed 'Duchess' after an incident when the (then) Duke of Portland asked to be introduced to her at some party they were both attending. She was very delicate as a child with severe anaemia, and was sent by her doctor to the seaside at Margate on the east coast of England which was considered *the* place to go in those days to recuperate. She was put in a wheel-chair and fed on plenty of tomatoes and raw beef! The treatment certainly seemed to help, as in later years she was a good tennis player, a good ballroom dancer, and followed the Beagle hounds when hunting hares.

Beagle hounds are short-legged hounds, sometimes called 'harriers'. Many years later I also followed the Beagles and found running over ploughed fields very hard on the ankles. The fields of England are deep-ploughed in very heavy loam leaving furrows in the soil that are very difficult to navigate.

My father, Alan Sim Murray, was a Captain at that time in the 2nd Battalion Sherwood Foresters — Nottinghamshire and Derbyshire Regiment (as it was then). He came from a family of five boys and two girls — Shakespear, Queenie, Lillymaid, Wyndham, Alan (my father), Richmond the youngest, and William who died as a child.

My father and mother were married at St. Botolph's Church, Colchester, Essex on 22nd October 1902, at the end of the Boer War.

They had planned a honeymoon in the Lake District — the home of the Hardens — but orders came for my father to join his regiment in Peking and a few weeks after their marriage they sailed on the P. & O. *Formosa* on December 13th, 1902 for China.

In those days life was gay with Legation parties and dinners. Present at these functions were the Consuls and representatives of many nations, and many interesting names appear on my parents visitors list.

It was etiquette to 'call' on other members of the community and the 'call' had to be returned. In the case of a bachelor one returned his 'call' by an invitation to dinner or drinks. When 'calling' on a married couple, usually at about 3.30 p.m. three of your cards were placed on a salver presented to you by a servant, namely two of your husband's, one each for the man and his wife, and one of your own for the wife. This custom was still in force when I lived in China.

A sample of my mother's visiting list is as follows:

Mr. W. J. Oudendijk —	Dutch Legation
Col. de Doobor-Mousnitski —	du 128 Chausseur E.S.
Mr. Kynard Hawdon —	1st Punjab Cavalry
Mr. R. G. Peck —	27th U.S. Infantry
Mr. and Lady Susan Townly —	Brit. Legation
R. Stukeley St. John —	40th Pathans
Mons. Louis Roussel —	French Guard
Sir Robert Hart —	Inspector General Imperial Chinese Customs
Maj. Drake Brockman —	5th Bengal Light Infantry
Freiherr von Mumm —	Kaiserlicher Gesandter
Rev. Norris — (who baptised me)	Anglican Mission
Mons. et Mme. Yasuya Uchida—	Envoy Extrordinaire Ministre Plenipotentiaire de I. Majesty l'Empereur du Japan

At one big dinner party my mother fainted and came round to see a Russian doctor filling his mouth with water to blow in her face. She recovered quickly!

I have an old diary of my father's which he started on 13th December, 1902 — the day they sailed from Tilbury Docks, London. Unfortunately he has only entered very brief daily happenings of their slow trip to Peking — very typical of his methodical and 'to the point' mind. Example:-

24th Dec./02 "Arrived at Malta. Spent the day ashore, sailed during the night."

17th Jan./03 "Arrived at Penang. Spent the day ashore and sailed in the evening."

Very frustrating when one would love to have a more detailed picture!

They arrived in Hong Kong on 27th January and stayed a fortnight before leaving for Shanghai on the Canadian Pacific Co's *'Empress of India'*. From Shanghai they proceeded on the Chinese M & M Company's ship 'Kwang Ping' to Ching-wan-Tao — then by train to Tientsin, where they stayed the night and next day went on by train to Peking:- "Arriving on 27th Feb. about 6.30 p.m. Col. & Mrs. Bowers put us up till the night of Thursday 5th March when we entered our quarters in the Legation Grounds." I can imagine how tired my mother must have been and glad to be in their own quarters.

There is then a gap in the diary till:-

July 7th "I went down to Tientsin to meet Lina."

July 8th "Went to Tongku early. *"Eldorado"* not arrived. Stayed at Station Hotel."

July 9th " *"Eldorado"* passed Tongku in afternoon. I boarded Customs boat. Stayed night on board."

July 10th "Took Lina up to Peking arriving 1.30 p.m."

Here ended my father's diary to my knowledge!

Tongku is a small town at the mouth of the river going up to Tientsin where the pilot and custom station were situated. There were also Chinese fortifications at Tongku guarding the entrance to the river.

When my arrival was imminent, my aunt Lina Harden came from England to be with my mother. On board she met a man who wanted to marry her, but she was too frightened of men to take the plunge and sadly she never married. She played a very great family part right through my childhood in every facet of my life, and I owe much to her for the love, affection and interest she gave me.

My birth should have taken place at the British Legation, Peking, but erysipelas broke out and two days before I was born the doctor moved my mother to a British mission outside the Legation Quarter. She was carried in a sedan-chair by four stalwart Chinese — wondering where she was going and what was in store for her. So I was born in a small mission house with paper windows, to a mother full of fear, even of my father's Chinese servant, who slept outside her door to protect her when my father was away. She was in a very different China to the one I was to know, enjoy and love in later years.

Начальникъ и Общество Офицеровъ Пекинскаго Посольскаго Охраннаго Отряда покорнѣйше просятъ Поручика Алана Сим-Мюррэй съ Супругой пожаловать на музыкальный вечеръ и ужинъ, имѣющіе быть 22 Марта с.г. (4 Апр.) въ 9½ г. вечера, въ помѣщеніи Пекинскаго клуба.

Le Colonel de Dovbor-Mousnitski et les officiers de la Garde de la Légation Impériale Russe à Pékin prient Madame et Monsieur le lieutenant Alan-Sim-Murray St. For.
de leur faire l'honneur de vouloir bien venir à la soirée musicale et au souper, qui auront lieu ce 4 Avril au Peking-Club, à 9½ du soir.

R.S.V.P.

Invitation written in Russian and French from the Imperial Russian Legation to a soiree at the Peking Club at 9.30 p.m.

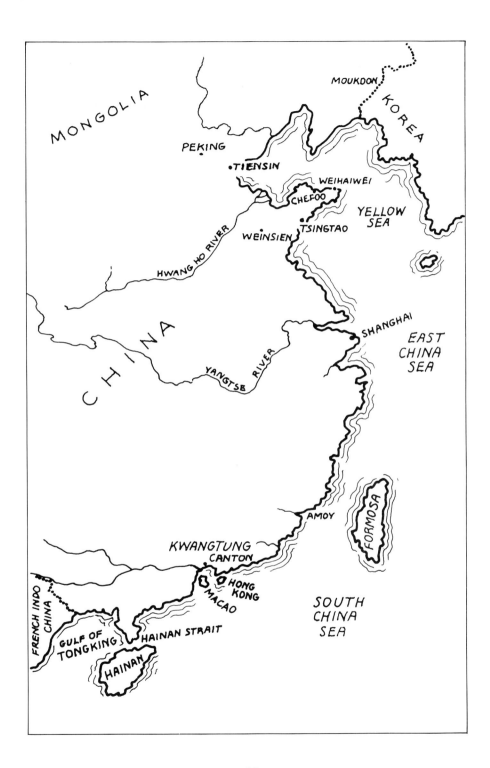

MONGOLIA

MOUKDON

KOREA

PEKING

•TIENSIN

WEIHAIWEI

CHEFOO

YELLOW
SEA

HWANG HO RIVER

WEINSIEN

TSINGTAO

CHINA

SHANGHAI

EAST
CHINA
SEA

YANGTSE RIVER

FORMOSA

AMOY

KWANGTUNG
CANTON

FRENCH INDO CHINA

HONG
KONG

MACAO

SOUTH
CHINA
SEA

GULF OF
TONGKING

HAINAN STRAIT

HAINAN

Sep 1st

Dear Murray,

The Empress Dowager having sent to inquire what the names of the legation ladies were I took the liberty of christening

Mrs Murray, 慕 Mu Taitai,
Miss Murray, " " Kuniang
& Miss Harden, 哈 Ha Kuniang

I hope they wont disapprove

Yours truly
R. Wilkinson

Letter from British Legation Peking 1903, giving mother, aunt and author (just arrived) our Chinese names.

27th July 1903 — Mother in sedan chair 2 days before author was born.

Mission House Peking where author was born.

I was christened by the Rev. Frank L. Norris at the British Legation Chapel, Peking. My names were Alice Rosaline after both of my grandmothers. I eventually became known as 'Little Alice' as it was confusing with three generations called 'Alice' in the immediate family. This eventually had to be given up when, at 15, I had grown to 5ft 8''.

In 1895 a secret society had been formed to rid China of all foreigners. The name 'BOXER'' was a translation of the Chinese name for the Society — I Ho Chi Uan (Righteous Harmony Fist), which initiated the Boxer Rising of 1900. The missionaries became an easy target as they were scattered throughout the country and had been connected, unfortunately, with the acquisition of territory by foreign powers, and the Society became anti-missionary as well as anti-foreign, and was in fact first forcibly brought to the notice of the British Government by the murder of a Mr. Brooks, a British Missionary.

The Boxer atrocities of 1902 were too recent for my mother not to be very conscious of them. Also there was much trouble in many parts of China at that period between the warring War Lords of the different provinces. So it was understandable that she felt much fear.

During my parents time in Peking the Empress used to send gifts to the 'ladies of the regiment' at various intervals. When I appeared, I was counted as one of those 'ladies' along with my mother and aunt!

Each lady received two gifts. One of the gifts commonly sent were large papier-mache containers, usually lacquered red with gold Imperial Dragons — much used in China at that time. These were filled with Chinese cakes and sweetmeats, but as the Empress was alleged to have indulged in atrocities the wives were forbidden to eat them for fear of being poisoned. Another gift sent to our house was six beautiful porcelain fern bowls on blackwood stands — two each for my mother and aunt and two for me! I have a very beautiful one still in my possession — much mended after many moves to many homes over the years. The others have disappeared with the exception of one that my brother has and which is in perfect condition, but without the blackwood stand.

Not very long after I was born my father had the chance of an 'exchange' and return to England. My mother was overjoyed as she had never liked China. She packed hurriedly to catch the last ship leaving Tientsin in time to get down the river before it was frozen over. That was the end of the papier-mache boxes as my mother stood on them while frantically taking down curtains and broke them. The ship edged her way down the river by tying a rope round the houses on the bank and being winched along, breaking the ice as she went. My mother

Empress T'zu Tse — the last Empress of China.

Chinese bowl in author's possesion given by the Empress T'zu Tse.

Lina and Alice outside their quarters.

Alice's drawing room, Peking.

and aunt were very bad sailors and too sick to bath and care for me so the job fell to my father who, I am told, performed the operation with somebody holding the bath on the table — not very easy in a rough sea! Perhaps that had something to do with my own unseaworthiness.

My father was stationed in the Isle of Wight when we first returned to England but my very first memories were of Nottingham, where we were later stationed when I was about three.

It was in Nottingham that I saw my first motor-car — an amazing affair belonging to a friend. My mother seemed to be sitting very high above me enveloped in a large white veil covering her hat and tied under her chin. It must have been a very early model car — about 1905-6.

Both families of grandparents, the Murrays and the Hardens, lived at Colchester in my early years — I suppose because it was a garrison town and had been since Roman times, also both grandfathers had been in the Army and retired there — one was a Colonel in an Infantry Regiment and the other was a Surgeon-General from the University of Aberdeen, Scotland. Both grandfathers are buried in the old churchyard in the village of Shrub End — now almost a part of metropolitan Colchester.

My Harden ancestory came from a mixed marriage of Irish from Borrisoleigh, Co. Tipperary and Scottish from Edinburgh. They wanted to settle somewhere between Ireland and Scotland and chose Brathay Hall on Lake Windermere. One of the sons married a girl called Angelina Salusbury and through this marriage came my Italian ancestry. Mrs. Thrale (nee Salusbury), a close friend of the 18th century writer Dr. Samuel Johnson, married a musician called Piozzi after her first husband died and adopted his young red-haired nephew, later to be known as Sir John Salusbury-Piozzi-Salusbury, the father of Angelina. Many years later we linked ourselves with this past romance by calling our house in Western Australia 'Brynbella' meaning 'Beautiful Valley' and combining Welsh and Italian. Unfortunately our Australian house in no way resembled the lovely old mansion built in 1794 by the Piozzis at St. Asaph, Flintshire, that we visited in 1972 — with its 'Lodge' cottage — beautiful iron gates and weathercock on the gable of the stables. A Georgian house of grey stone from the front and from the garden at the back one looked up at an Italianate facade — quite a remarkable combination. The house was built on sloping ground which meant there were two stories in front and three at the back. The house is still marked on the map as 'Brynbella' and the meaning at least suited our Australian house.

I went to stay with my Harden grandparents at Colchester in 1908 where my brother Bill was born just before my fifth birthday. One morning my Aunt Lina took me to Aunt Jessie to play in her garden. Aunt Jessie lived all her married life at 3, Queens Road, Colchester and was the only member of the family who did not constantly move house, so I remember her home from very early days. After a while I can remember the two aunts saying they thought it would all be over and we could return to my grandparents. I was then taken upstairs to my mother's room to see my brother for the first time — a small red body having his flannel binder sewn on by the nanny, as was the custom at that time. A 'flannel binder' is a strip of flannel about 4''wide — wrapped round the baby's middle and sewn up down the back. It was left on until the umbiblical cord was healed. I do not know the medical reason for discontinuing this practice.

I remember one day, when I was being taken for a walk, seeing the road covered with straw in front of a house and asking why it was like this. I was told that somebody was very ill in that house and the straw on the road was to deaden the sound of the carriage or cart wheels and the horses shoes on the road so as not to disturb the sick person. The disturbing noise of traffic on built-up roads is still a problem today.

Some years later, at the age of twelve, I was to go to my first school in Colchester run by a Miss Harley. I do not know that I learnt very much, but I do remember having a very happy time there and made my first friend with a girl called Rosalind Slaughter. One day we decided to go 'trespassing' on our bicycles. She knew of a country house whose owners had gone away on holiday. So off we went and pushed our way through the garden gate to investigate. Suddenly we heard heavy footsteps coming down the path and ran for our lives, I think it was the gardener, whom we had not reckoned with! Our second effort at 'trespassing' was to climb a hill with a large haystack at the top and go up a ladder propped at the side. We were enjoying ourselves and the lovely view till we suddenly spotted the irate farmer running across the field brandishing a pitchfork. This really frightened us and we slid down the opposite side of the haystack as fast as we could and onto our bicycles and away, after which we decided we had had enough 'trespassing'. I always hoped we had not damaged the farmer's haystack too much!

In later years, my mother's sister Janie married a Doctor Harwood-Yarred practising in Colchester, a one-time president of the Royal College of Surgeons. He lived and practised in the historical and beautiful old house called Tymperleys, which had been a doctors house since the time of Queen Elizabeth I, and where, I understand, she stayed when she went to visit her physician. In a small room, converted to a bathroom off my aunt's bedroom, was a very high corner cupboard believed to have been used for the Queen's wigs. When we stayed there to get to our bedroom we had to go down a low roofed passage so narrow that it was impossible to carry a tray down it. During World War II this house was much photographed by the American Soldiers who were stationed at Colchester as it was one of the best preserved Elizabethan houses in the area. The last time I saw Tymperleys in 1972, it had been beautifully restored and I understand that the present owner has left it to the town. It stands right in the centre of old Colchester.

Our next posting was to Fermoy in County Cork, Ireland. We went up to London to catch the train to Fishguard and we drove through the dark London streets at night in a horse-drawn cab with the cabby sitting on a high seat at the back. It all seemed very mysterious to a six-year-old. At the Paddington Railway Hotel I experienced my first late dinner and the waiter tying what seemed to be a huge stiff white dinner napkin round my neck and putting in front of me an equally huge plate of soup which I felt sure was the cause of my subsequent seasickness when crossing the Irish sea, but that was proved incorrect as the years went by and I was equally seasick without the soup.

On arrival at Fermoy we were taken up the hill to the barracks, where we were to live in the Adjutant's house. My mother, brother, nanny and self were hoisted on to a 'jaunting car', a peculiarly Irish conveyance, being a high two-wheeled vehicle with seats back to back in the centre facing outwards and the driver in front. I remember the sensation of feeling very precarious with my mother's arm holding me on one side and the other arm clutching on to nanny and my brother on the other side. I have a vivid recollection of the green-painted walls on the stairway of the four-storey house we lived in and how on damp days these walls trickled with moisture. In enjoyed looking out of the nursery window at the top of the house, watching the regiment parade on the barrack square below.

My brother's nanny adored him, but not me, and one afternoon while wheeling him round the barrack square in his pram she resented my walking beside it so made me run round and round on my own. After I had been round a few times I was rescued by the General's wife who went next door to report to my mother what was happening!

Happily I was saved more discriminatory treatment by the fact that the dampness of Southern Ireland did not agree with me, so it was decided to send me back to Colchester with Aunt Lina to stay with my grandparents, then living in a nice old house in the village of Shrub End with a marvellous garden and a huge fir tree that I played under for hours — planning houses by sweeping the fronds that fell so thickly to form the different rooms of my house! There were two large cherry trees and a big vegetable and flower garden and lovely strawberries and cream at the tennis parties under the trees. It was a beautiful warm summer and I can still picture it all very clearly.

One day that winter the daily paper arrived with a thick black line round the pages and news of the death of King Edward VII. There was a lot of talk and speculation, so we decided to go into Colchester in the pony cart to hear the 'latest' but before we did that a black hat had to be found for me! We eventually set off with me wearing my white winter coat with an extraordinary black hat and black armband.

My father had 'second sight'. It was not a thing that he dabbled in but it just happened to be so. One day in Ireland he rode over on his bicycle to visit a Mrs. Beecher who lived in a very large old house near Fermoy and riding up the drive he saw a maid whom he had not seen before picking flowers. He said to Mrs. Beecher ''I see you have a new maid''. The family looked at each other puzzled, then Mrs. Beecher said ''Oh that would be Mary''. They had names for the various ghosts that haunted the place.

They also had a locked room that was never opened and the window of which was overgrown with ivy. My father was anxious to climb up a ladder and look in, but they would not let him. One day I was taken to see Mrs. Beecher and she told me a story about a little girl with red hair who used to come and play in the garden every winter. I must have sensed something strange in the story as I remember feeling so very frightened. I learnt later that it was one of their family ghosts that she was telling me about, though she never said so to me.

Some years later my father had a very strange experience. The regiment was under canvas at Willsworthy Down, Devonshire — a very bleak part of Dartmoor not far from Dartmoor prison. He was settling down in his campbed for the night and turned to pull his bedding over his shoulder when he saw a yellow hand hovering over him — he dodged and it disappeared. He got up to make sure that the tent fly was secure thinking that the hand might belong to an escaped prisoner. As he did this there was a terrible commotion two tents away. When he investigated he found an officer called Jackson crouched down with his bedclothes strewn everywhere saying that ''something'' had tried to strangle him, but there was nobody there. Every explanation was put forward, such as a late party — moonlight reflection — but nothing fitted. It was discovered later that a band of people had once been massacred on that spot many years ago. Stranger still — after the first World War at an evening party when guests were asked to recount a true ghost story, my father's eldest brother Shakespear told this story and when he had finished one of the women present said "That is very strange, I was going to tell the same story about my fiance". It transpired her fiance had been the Jackson of the original experience. He had been killed in the 1914-18 war.

You can believe this story or not, as you wish. My father was a fearless person, not at all given to imagining things and as I have said, he never dabbled in the occult, but he was 'fey' as are many Scots.

When my parents returned from Ireland in about 1910, our next posting was to Crown Hill just outside Plymouth (or it was then). The mascot of the regiment was an old ram who on church parade wore a most beautifully embroidered coat, worked by the wives of the regiment. He was led by two soldiers whose special job it was to look after him, and it was a proud moment for the old ram with the band playing and all the fanfares. He was too old at that time to march far but he managed to lead them as far as the bottom of the hill and then the Regiment marched on to the barracks. It was all very colourful, the Regiment in their red coats, blue trousers and shining buttons and the band playing.

The Regiments mascot had been a ram since the time of the Indian Mutiny when, in 1858, the commanding officer had noticed a fine fighting ram by a temple. He commandered the ram which was named Derby 1. It marched contentedly with the Regiment for 3,000 miles and was in six 'actions' in Central India. He received, equally with the Battalion in 1862, the 'India Medal' with clasp for Central India which is now in the Regimental Museum in Derby, England.

I went to my first big children's party at Christmas given by the Navy in Plymouth dockyard. They gave us a most marvelous time, as only the Navy can, fishing for pennies in electrified water and all sorts of exciting things quite new to me.

My father decided in 1912 to retire from the Army as promotion was very slow. We left Crown Hill on my ninth birthday and moved to a new life in a house called Bramblemoor in the village of Broadhempston, Devon. My parents took on the usual rural village life and we were fairly self-supporting with a vegetable garden and poultry. They used to go to tennis parties on their bicycles; we went

1911. Crownhill, Devon. The Mascot of the 2nd Batt. Sherwood Foresters after Church Parade.

on lovely walks down the lanes covered with primroses and daffodils in the spring, and in the summer picnics up Hay Tor in the village trap owned and driven by a man called Vallance.

Sometimes we had our Harden cousins staying with us; and driving home from picnics through the narrow Devonshire lanes, we could touch the hedges on each side, and we played 'Up Jenkins' with a rug stretched over our knees from one side of the trap to the other, something we all enjoyed and remember to this day.

My brother and I had a governess and I started regular lessons for the first time. I spent much time collecting birds eggs from the Devonshire hedges — it was my 'collecting' period — eggs — butterflies — crests — stamps. My stamps I carried on for many years and later started a collection for my daughter Patricia at the time of the Silver Jubilee of King George V, but they were unfortunately all lost during World War II. I often wish I had started again after the war as stamps have always interested me.

Broadhempston was a happy period in my life. The house had lovely old stables — a garden with trees to climb — an old 'mounting block' built into the garden wall with steps into the garden and a tiny iron gate at the top where I spent hours playing imaginative games by myself. There were dogs to go for walks, picnics in the field opposite after they had cut the hay, and drives with Mr. Vallance to childrens' parties in nearby villages. Two young friends — twins Geraldine and Algy May — used to ride over on their moor ponies bare-back from Staverton, our nearest railway. They were expert riders and did not hesitate to put me on a pony's back and give it a good whack to make it rear up, which terrified me as I had never ridden a horse in those days, much less bare-back! Geraldine was into every scrape she could think of and her thick blue serge dress was bound with brown leather to preserve it's life. Their father, Admiral May, must have had a hard time with a family of five, two sets of twins and one lonely girl in the middle.

At Bramblemoor we had a flock of white fantail pigeons which had their home in the stable loft. It was delightful to hear them billing and cooing and to watch them swooping round at certain times of the day. I wonder if their offspring are still flying around there?

Also at Bramblemoor we had two dogs with very different characteristics. The senior was called 'Bob' an old-fashioned black-and-white wire-haired terrier, and a great fighter. The junior was twice his size — an adorable grey and white Old English sheepdog called 'Gunner'. I was given the job of keeping him brushed and could just squeeze him onto a narrow seat in the old trellissed porch by the front door for this operation. He sat there so good while I tried to comb out the mats of hair like felt, but often I had to resort to cutting them out. He was a very sweet natured dog and followed Bob everywhere, even when on our walks Bob would rush into some farmyard gate and engage the farm dogs in a fight. Gunner would join in and it was a great job to separate them all. When we did, the dogs who had bitten Gunner had 'beards' from the hair they had bitten off him, but Gunner was unscathed and enjoyed the fun. Sadly he went blind at a very early age due to my paternal grandmother cutting the hair that fell over his eyes thinking that he would see better. She had not realized that the purpose of this fringe was to protect his sensitive eyes.

At the beginning of the First World War, we gave temporary home to three of my Harden cousins, Jessie, Kannie and Margot. Their father, Uncle Jack, and my father had both re-joined their regiments. As there were five children living in the house we decided to put on a play to raise money for the war effort and asked a friend living in the village called Peggy d'Alton to join us, our ages ranged between twelve and five. The schoolroom was a lovely long room running over the harness and store rooms so we had a perfect setting. As far as I can remember we all did various dances in different national and Grecian style costumes which we had made up ourselves — all except Bill's kilt which we decided fitted Peggy d'Alton better than him, he was dressed as Peter Pan. Peggy and the aunt she lived with were Irish and the aunt was most upset that we should dress her niece in a Scottish kilt! It nearly started another war but somehow the problem was smoothed over. My mother's friends came to see our production and we ended by raising a few shillings and had a lot of fun.

Because of the war it became necessary for us to move again and we 'let' Bramblemoor to a Belgian refugee and his sister for a very nominal rent and they were to look after our two dogs, Gunner and Bob, whom we were unable at that time to take with us. We were not able to get the Belgians turned out, until the end of the war. They refused to hand over the dogs or make any move. They kept themselves shut up and the big gates to the cobbled yard were always locked. My father went down one day as soon as he was free — put his hand under the gates and the dogs gave him a great welcome. Somehow he got in and took the dogs away. We heard many odd stories from people in the village after the war. They were convinced that the Belgians had been spies.

Sadly we never went back to live at Bramblemoor. My brother visited it in recent years and it is much the same, a delightful little house.

Chapter 2

SCHOOL-DAYS AND MARRIAGE

War is a most disruptive element in ones life. Bill and I needed educating and it was decided that we should live in Exmouth, Devon, away from the bombs and where there were good schools for us to go to daily. I went to 'Southlands' a large girls' school whose head mistress was a Miss Fearon with the most piercing blue eyes I have ever seen. Her name seemed very apt. My brother went to a Preparatory school for boys called St. Peters.

At this time my mother and Aunt Lina used to take us to farms in North Devon or Somerset for our summer holidays. One farm we stayed at in North Devon was very short of labour due to the war and was glad of any help. I learnt to milk a Devonshire cow whose tail was the same copper colour as my hair and used to get so tangled you could not distinguish the difference — or so I was told! I also helped on the haystack, all of which I enjoyed and it made me feel quite important.

Two holidays we spent at an old and primitive farm at Withypool on the Somerset moors near Dulverton in the 'Lorna Doone' country. The farm was not very far from Hardacre Bridge mentioned in the book. The son was about 16 and tried to base his life on John Ridd the hero in 'Lorna Doone'. The farmer's wife gave us large bowls of Somerset clotted cream at every meal and delicious fried mashed potato and bacon for breakfast. We washed in small bowls of soft smokey rain-water. When the lamps were lit in the evening the farmer would bring large slabs of peat over his shoulder, about three feet long and over a foot wide, to throw on the fire in the large old hearth. The smell was lovely and it sparkled and spat as one fanned the fire with huge old bellows.

If one went into the kitchen in the evening one would see the farmer sitting on a small stool inside the huge stone fireplace cracking hazelnuts which grew profusely on the hedges, a great iron kettle would be hanging on an iron hook over the fire, and the farmer's wife was busy mashing potatoes in a bucket ready for breakfast in the morning. Outside in the dairy were large flat pans of milk 'setting' ready to skim for the clotted cream next day. Such a peaceful, simple life but the work was very hard in the cold and wet of a Somerset winter.

We used to go to many of the 'meets'. They hunted foxes, hares, and stags. I remember going quite a long way to a 'meet' of the famous Somerset staghounds. We borrowed a moor pony from the farm and my Aunt Lina, my brother and myself took it in turns to ride or run. The little moor ponies are strong and sturdy but I think this one must have had quite an exhausting day! We had a marvelous day although we did not see a stag. I understand stag hunting in Britain has now been stopped and I am glad these proud animals are left in peace.

The country was very beautiful with the hedges of hazelnuts, masses of lovely heather and here-and-there bogs of sphagnum moss, a pale green moss that grows in the bogs and was collected and used for making dressings for the war effort. I understand it has some curative properties. I have often wondered if it is the same kind of moss used by the American Indians to line the moccasin-shaped cradles in which they put their 'papoose' and strap on their backs.

Another year we went by train to a place called South Molton and decided to bicycle from there to Withypool. We were pushing our bicycles up a hill and came on a group of prisoners mending the road. One of them had 'BLUCHER' on his cap. This famous ship was sunk by the British Navy in the battle of Jutland in World War I, one of the famous battles of naval history. The sight of these men made a great impression on us children.

During this time my father was still on active service. He was attached to the 9th Battalion Sherwood Foresters, his old regiment having gone to France. In July 1915 they were camped under canvas at Frensham Ponds, Surrey, waiting for embarkation. My mother, Bill and I went to Frensham from London to say goodbye. We stayed in rather uncomfortable rooms to be near the camp. The dreaded day came, and during the night I awoke to hear my mother crying, and then I heard the tramp of many feet on the road below and the band playing very softly as the Regiment marched past, many never to return from a tragic episode in the 1914-18 war. It was an experience I will never forget — a feeling of sadness for all these men marching into the unknown with such brave hearts and the anxiety and loneliness of the families they left behind.

They embarked at Liverpool during the first week in July 1915 on the *Empress of Britain* and took part in the devasting landing at Suvla

Bay, Gallipoli as part of the 11th Division at the beginning of August 1915. Later he was very badly wounded; the bullet passing through the side of his neck and coming out near the spine. He lay on the hot bleak hillside for sometime till a fellow officer found him and came to his aid. My father always said that the Turks were true 'sportsmen' in the way they fought and would not hesitate to bring back a wounded enemy to his own lines, and we would do the same for them, both sides stopping the firing. War is conducted differently today.

My father left the Greek islands and bays that he thought so beautiful and returned home in a hospital ship to the Endsleigh Palace Hotel, Leicester Square, which had been turned into a military hospital. I went there once with my mother to see him. He still had his arm in a sling and the doctor told him he was lucky to be alive as the bullet had passed through very vital parts of the neck.

When he recovered sufficiently, he was posted to the command of a large establishment on the North East Coast, where Officers and WAAC'S (Womens Auxiliary Army Corps) who had been sick or wounded were accommodated for re-training. He continued to command various depots in the north of England until the Armistice and saw no more active service.

When the bombing stopped we moved to London as the war was nearing an end. In the autumn term of 1918, just before the Armistice was signed, I went to a small boarding school at Hindhead, Surrey, called Twizzletwig (much to everyone's amusement) which meant 'hill between two valleys', and my brother went to Lancing College in Sussex where my father had been before him. I wish I had worked harder whilst at Twizzletwig and not wasted my own and everyone else's time. I loved it there and for the first time made friends that I have kept over the years and with whom I still correspond.

The first friend I made was Marjorie Chignell. One of her aunts was the headmistress and her parents lived in India. She took up secretarial work when she left school and was a senior secretary with Eversharp Pen Co. for 25 years, surely quite a record. Marjorie still lives in London and we last met in 1972 when I went to England.

Patricia Wallace, the daughter of Edgar Wallace, author of 'Bones' and 'People of the River' and many thrillers was also at Twizzletwig. We were great friends although she was several years younger than me. She adored her father and their letters to each other were wonderfully illustrated with little drawings and verses. She was a clever girl and later went on to Cheltenham College and we lost touch. Edgar Wallace often came down to see Pat at weekends and stayed at the

Hindhead Hotel close to the school. I find it hard to describe him after so many years.

I was 15 when I knew him and my memory is of a man of medium height, rather round, racey, kindly, and always busy, full of imagination, always with a long cigarette holder, and devoted to Pat. He often invited me out with her when he came to Hindhead. Sometimes he would bring his secretary who later became his wife.

At that time I suffered very badly from broken chilblains on my hands and had great difficulty washing my face when both hands were bandaged. I remember Pat doing this job for me with great skill. One weekend her father brought some Grasshopper Ointment as an 'instant cure' for my chilblains and I was thrilled by the possibility. Unfortunately something went wrong, an infection developed with one finger and I still have the scar. The whole Wallace family were wonderful to me and used to bring back chocolates and gifts from Switzerland, where they went every year for the Christmas holiday to stay at the, then, Palace Hotel at Caux. When I left school I was invited to their flat in Portland Place, London and met some of their theatrical friends. I could not understand my mother's obvious concern about who I was likely to meet! It was certainly a very different world to that which I had been used to and an insight into an interesting and vital way of life. Edgar Wallace started earning his living as a newspaper boy and rose to being a millionaire and a world-famous author and playright.

Another school friend was Margot Anderson from Jersey. Her maternal grandmother was a Mrs. Lodge, cousin of the well-known, eccentric Oliver Lodge. She had married a first cousin, also a Lodge. She was a delightful elderly lady who had been a widow for many years. She always wore grey or violet-coloured long moire silk dresses and lived with a bachelor son at Witley, not far from Hindhead. Margot and I sometimes went from school to stay weekends with her. It was a large house with lovely garden and grounds, and a swimming pool, an unusual acquisition in those days. Mrs. Lodge dearly loved this house. One evening she took me to a paddock on top of a hill to watch the sunset, a thing she very much enjoyed doing. She had a wooden seat built round a tree so that she could sit watching the sunset in comfort — and there we sat together. Later when they sold the house and moved to Rickmansworth she often asked me to go and stay for the weekend — pleasant break for me from London. She still wore stiff silk dresses that rustled as she moved — she enjoyed reading Edgar Wallace's African books — 'Bones' and 'The People of the

River' and used to read them to me in the evening.

Several years later I heard from Margot of two occasions when she 'returned' after she had died. The first was when a grand-daughter was having a difficult 'labour' and Mrs. Lodge appeared at the foot of the bed. From that moment the birth proceeded without any more difficulty. The other occasion was most interesting to me. The people who bought the house at Witley decided to sell it after living there for a while. They had never met Mrs. Lodge but gave their reasons for selling as the fact that a little old lady would suddenly appear in the room, bustle through in her silk dress and disappear, and sometimes they would see her sitting on the wooden seat under the tree watching the sunset! They said she was quite peaceful but they found her sudden appearance disturbing. The description they gave to the agent was of Mrs. Lodge!! She had returned to the place she loved so much. I hope she still goes to her tree where we watched the sunset in such peace together — the delightful old lady in her silks and the teenager with her long auburn pigtails.

One summer holiday I was invited by my friend Nancy Pears (also a student at Twizzletwig), to stay with her on her parents farm at Waddington Heath, Lincolnshire. For me, to stay with a large family, with lots of friends and lots of fun was a wonderful experience. Peggy was the eldest, then Betty who was married and came with her husband to visit. The two sisters had been 'land girls' during World War I, and Betty was the beauty of the family. Next came George, the only son, and the youngest was my friend Nancy.

I travelled from London by train and was met by Mr. Pears and Nancy in a most wonderful old car — worth a fortune nowadays. There were two seats in front up a high step and the back was rounded like a governess-cart with a door at the rear. My luggage was loaded and off we went. When travelling I always liked to have everything with me that I might need, and I think the amount of my luggage rather astonished the Pears family and ever after George used to refer to me as the 'lodger'. I spent seven consecutive summers holidaying with the family and have always felt one of them.

The Pears' farm was called 'Glebe Farm'. It belonged to the Church as all 'Glebe' land did. The farmhouse was a very old three-storey Queen Anne building superimposed on a much earlier crofter's cottage — more or less one room up and one room down. The back part of the house, when I knew it, was called the 'back kitchen'. It was first lived in by the Pears' family when it was rented to Nancy's grandfather in 1870 and bought by her father in 1920, making their occupation well over 100 years. The ceilings were very low and I could reach them with my wrist, and it was very important to 'duck' going through a doorway in a 2ft thick wall between the front and back of the house.

Waddington Heath is a very old district historically. There is a Roman road following the prehistoric trackway — this passed across the end of the Pears' property. 'Waddington' meant the 'tun' (that is, the township of the Waddings — followers of a Chieftain called Wadder). It was a group of 'tuns' that grew up round the old Roman city of Lincoln early in the 7th century. In the 9th century the Danish Kings made Lincoln a garrison borough and the countryside was influenced by Scandinavian dialects and customs — with Danish names such as 'Colby' and 'Nazenby'.

Waddington is known throughout the world because of its R.A.F. station which came into being in 1917 as a training post for the then R.F.C. (Royal Flying Corps). Through the dark days of 1939 and 1945 it was one of the foremost operational stations under Bomber Command. The first bombing mission of the war was made from Waddington on 3rd September, 1939. After the war Waddington remained a bomber base returning to a peacetime training routine. Many years later I was to meet men in Australia who had flown from Waddington R.A.F. Station.

The last time I stayed at the Pears' home was in 1972 with Peggy who, with her sister Betty are the only members of that generation still alive. The family had a very bad time during World War II as Waddington airfield was under constant attack. The farmhouse was within a couple of miles from the airfield and 'near-misses' came very close at times.

The period from 1920 onwards was a difficult time financially for my parents, and sadly I had to leave school just before my 17th birthday. We were living in a maisonette (2 floors in a 4-storey house) near Hampstead Heath. We had the ground-floor and basement which meant we had a small garden at the back. Our rooms were nice and large, having been the living rooms when a private house, but it seemed so dingy after the country. Civilian jobs were very few and far between at the end of demobilization, but my father was fortunate to get a job as secretary to the Royal National Lifeboat Institution. The job involved money-raising and this was something he did not like being so different from what he had been used to in the army, but he stuck it out for a few years until at least one of us was earning a living.

We enjoyed the walks over Hampstead Heath, and one evening after work my father called on Sir Gerald du Maurier, the well-known and popular actor, to enlist his help financially in a Lifeboat Institution project, and took me with him. Sir Gerald lived in a beautiful house on the far side of the Heath, near the historical 'Jack Straw's Castle'. We were shown into a very delightful room facing the slope where we used to toboggan when there was snow. The room gave one a sense of peace and warmth with its soft shaded lights and pleasant furnishings. Sir Gerald was standing with his back to the fire with all his family present, three daughters, namely Angela, Daphne and Jane, and Lady du Maurier sitting at her desk. At the time I thought the youngest was a 'boy' as 'he' was dressed in short trousers (not then worn by girls) and had short hair, but years later I discovered that 'he' was in fact the third girl who always wanted to be a boy!

They all seemed to me to have golden hair which accentuated the soft golden atmosphere of the room. I felt very conspicuous standing there with my red hair. Daphne du Maurier became a well known author, following in the footsteps of her grandfather George du Maurier who wrote the classic 'Trilby'. I always enjoyed Gerald du Maurier's plays when I could afford to go to the theatre, and to have met him with his family in their delightful home gave me an added interest.

In those days there was always an annual dinner for the officers of the Sherwood Foresters and a reunion next day for their families at the Hyde Park Hotel. It was a very gay and friendly affair with General Sir Horace Smith-Dorrien G.C.B., G.C.M.G., D.S.O. (Col. of the Regiment) and Lady Smith-Dorrien D.B.E., always present. He was a very popular officer and highly professional soldier. He fought in many campaigns, with great distinction, in South Africa and in all the desperate battles in France in 1914. Lady Smith-Dorrien was the daughter of Colonel J. Schneider of Furness Abbey, Lancashire. Her family changed their name to 'Crofton' during the 1914-18 war. She was created a 'Dame' in 1916. Through her Hospital Bag Fund she had provided British and Colonial troops with some 8,000,000 hospital bags for the contents of wounded men's pockets. She received the gold medal of the Reconnaissance Francaise for her work for French horses through her Presidency of the Blue Cross. One of her brothers was a fellow officer of my father's.

The reunion was always held on a Saturday afternoon, and on the Sunday following we were invited to a tennis party at the lovely home of Col. and Mrs. Rhodes at Remenham near Henley-on-Thames. It always seemed to be a perfect summer day — the younger ones played tennis and the older ones talked over old times in the beautiful garden. In 1938, when my husband and I were on leave from China, we visited the Rhodes with my mother. We wandered through the old 'walled' garden and were interested to see the peach trees which were espaliered on a wall facing south. They said they fruited well although it is unusual to grow peaches outside a hot-house in England.

On leaving school my ambition was to be a gym mistress (Phys. Ed. these days), anything to do with sport and games, but not having taken my schooling seriously I had not matriculated. So I went instead to Madame Hoster's exclusive secretarial college in Grosvenor Place, London, and took a six-months course. Madame Hoster was quite a personality. She seldom appeared but when she did she was dressed in black with a black lace Elizbethan collar; she rolled her r's, looked very impressive, tall and stern. The six-months course took in the usual subjects — finishing with a month in Madame Hoster's office in the City of London. It was a good way to get her business done and a good finishing training for us! The standard of work was exceptionally high and concentrated, and she guaranteed a job in the field in which you were interested if you passed the course. The house overlooked the back of Buckingham Palace gardens and one could see right into the garden from the top floor, with the Palace in the distance. We used to sneak upstairs hoping to see some interesting event!

I was not long in getting a job, which I held for 8½ years. It was with a Harley Street throat-and-ear specialist, Mr. Andrew Wylie. He was brought up in Scotland and had never lost his Scottish accent. He was the middle man in a family of 13, and always said he was the 'odd man out' when it came to parties — too old for the youngest and too young for the eldest. They were made to keep strict Scottish sabbaths — to read only suitable books and go to 'kirk'.

The family were very good to me and gave me an insight into London society and events that I would not otherwise have experienced. Perhaps it was then that I acquired my love of beautiful and expensive clothes that I have never been able to afford!! Some Saturdays Mrs. Wylie took me to the famous clubs such as Hurlingham and Ranelagh — to have lunch and watch Polo, or she would give me tickets for Wimbledon, where I saw Suzanne Lenglen, 'Bunny' Austin and other great players of that time.

The Wylies always took a grouse 'shoot' in Scotland every August and one year invited me to go with them. It was certainly a very new experience for me in a large house on the moors in Kirkudbrightshire, miles from anywhere. When I went up to my room to dress for dinner I found a maid had unpacked my things and laid out the evening dress, shoes etc., she thought I should wear. Unfortunately it was a dress I did not like very much but felt I had to do the right thing! We used to play snooker after dinner, and when there was not a 'shoot' during the day there would be clay-pigeon shooting, marvellous picnics on the moors, or trout fishing — all of which I thoroughly enjoyed — except extricating the worms from one of those oldfashioned silver tobacco pouches which popped open when you squeezed it and the worms popped out; I don't like worms even today! We were usually a party of 6 with a ghillie, some beaters and the dogs. A day tramping over the moors was exhilarating and we were hungry for the delicious picnics brought in large hampers carried in panniers by a pony.

The world seemed full of joy and interest in those days — no forbodings of all the turmoils to follow — just there to be absorbed and enjoyed.

Mr. Wylie had a very varied clientele of patients, and I met many famous and well-known people among his regular patients during those years; such as the Earl of Strathmore, the Queen Mother's dignified and kindly father; her cousin the Hon. Nancy Bowes-Lyon; the ex-King George of Greece; Edith Day with the lovely voice and at that time the star in 'Show Boat' with Paul Robeson, singing songs such as "Why do I love you? — Why do you love me?" and Paul Robeson with his enormous bass singing the moving song "Old Man River".

Others who came were Heather Thatcher with her monocle, gay, vivacious, a fascinating musical comedy actress even off the stage; the two attractive Dare sisters, Phyllis and Zena, were also patients. About that time Zena married Lord Esher and for a time left the stage; and there were many more well-known personalities of the 1920 period.

Mr. Wylie always kept a bottle of 'Scotch' in a cupboard in his consulting room although he seldom drank from it himself. One year before I left for the Christmas break he called me in and said "Don't drink any of that whisky Miss Murray". I must have looked rather startled as it was something that I had never tasted in those days. He confided that he had noticed someone was habitually sampling his whisky and planned to put a stop to it by lacing the whisky with Epsom salts. The culprit was identified as the relief porter and he must have spent a very unhappy Christmas! My boss was a kindly man to work for, but he expected the best and was very meticulous and im-

About Aug. 1929. Andrew Wylie and author off fishing for trout,
Kirkcudbrightshire, Scotland.

patient of mistakes and bad spelling. He would find the present trend in the latter hard to understand.

My job consisted of attending to his correspondence, appointments, accounts and occasionally assisting in the consulting room by holding heads for small operations or treatments. The care and preparation of his operating bags for tonsilectomy or mastoids and the general care of all his instruments in the consulting room was my responsibility. Once a year, in the spring, he would go to Monte Carlo for a two-week gambling spree and invariably came back sick and in a very bad mood; but he always brought me back a lovely evening hand-bag. I spent the time he was away having a thorough spring-clean of drawers and cupboards etc., being very careful to put each instrument back in exactly the same place. I had had good training from my father who always knew if his dressing table had been dusted! I enjoyed those days of 'tidying up'.

Once a week Mr. Wylie used to treat patients at the out-patient's dept. at the E.N.T. hospital in Gray's Inn Road. I always went with him and sat on a chair at his right hand to fill in the patient's case-sheets. Behind us was always a group of students listening to his explanations — diagnosis — treatment — and his final instructions to me. I learnt a great deal by hearing what he said.

I was interested in, and took a great pride in my job, but 8½ years were exacting and money was always scarce. I worked hard when at home making all my clothes. I loved clothes and never enjoyed going out except in what I felt was 'right' for the occasion. On the dance floor I liked my dresses to look as glamorous as I could afford and in the country it had to be tweed skirts and brogues, but the prevailing rate for a job like mine was £3.10 per week with lunch and this did not go very far by the time I had given £1 a week towards my keep and paid for travelling to and from work.

120 Harley Street was at the Marylebone end, opposite my future husband's aunt — Dr. Ethel Vaughan-Sawyer the gynaecologist who lived at No. 131. Aunt Ethel Vaughan was the elder sister of my husband's mother. She was one of the early generation of women doctors in London, and married Major Harry Sawyer who was killed in the 1914-18 war. She was a most respected consultant and continued practising in her Harley Street home all through the blitz of World War II, having refused to leave even though the house was badly damaged.

Often I used to see the historic Dr. Mary Scharlieb walking past in her old fashioned coat and skirt of dark grey — one of the first woman doctors. Queen Victoria had expressed strong disapproval of women doctors, but her change of opinion was due to the brilliant colleague of Dr. Elizabeth Garret Anderson — namely Mary Scharlieb. She had practised in India and returned to England to take a higher degree at the London School of Medicine. The need was great in India for medical women as high-caste Indian ladies were not permitted to see a male doctor however dangerously ill they might be. Mary Scharlieb was appalled at the terrible suffering caused by this taboo and decided to become a doctor herself and study surgery. Queen Victoria, who always took a great interest in her Indian subjects, sent for Mary Scharlieb and questioned her about the need of the 40 million Indian women shut off from medical care. Mary was afraid she might be shocked at some of the details but the Queen insisted on the whole truth, and when she heard it exclaimed with feeling, "How could they tell me there is no need for medical women!" She gave Mary Scharlieb a signed photograph and told her to take it into her patient's homes when she returned to India to assure them how much their Queen felt for them.

Another interest was the Household Cavalry riding up Harley Street on their way to exercise in Regent's Park. They made a fine sight with their beautiful black horses, shining accoutrements and their large snow-white gauntlet gloves, and always brought a lump in my throat and a feeling of pride in their perfection.

I enjoyed the theatre when I got the chance. My favourites were musicals and I went as many as five times to see Maid of the Mountains from every different part of the theatre — from the stalls when I was taken, to the 'gods' when I paid for myself after standing in a queue for hours watching a man cutting paper pictures, or a performing monkey — all of which helped to pass the time.

One particular 'show' I enjoyed immensely was the first time I saw Fred Astaire and his sister Adele. They had just come from America and it was their debut on the London stage in 'Stop Flirting', doing the 'Oom-pah Trot' which received great applause. That was the only time I saw them dance together. Adele later married Lord Cavendish and left the stage. One night I was taken to the Cafe de Paris in Leicester Square after a dance — the rendezvous in those days of the theatre stars after their performances. This famous nightclub was destroyed in World War II by a bomb falling right through the centre of the glass ceiling and dance floor.

This was a period when I was taken by various boyfriends and cousins to see the Oxford and Cambridge boat race, the Aldershot

Tattoo, the Hendon Air Pageant, point-to-point races in the country, the Royal Artillery Ball at Greenwich known as the 'Shop' from which I arrived back in London with the milk and the Hunt Balls at Winchester. All these events I enjoyed and I am grateful to the friends and cousins who helped me to experience such a wonderful part of my life.

I was very fond of dancing and never missed an opportunity if I could help it. My great-aunt Jeanie (of whom more later) used to arrange parties of young people and take tickets for the big charity dances, mostly the Indian Empire Club dances at the Hyde Park Hotel. She never came herself. They were very glittering affairs and I enjoyed them. Once she invited me to her home after work to stay the night. I was taken to my room by her maid Reed — I changed and was ushered into the dining-room — expecting to see my aunt and guests — instead there was one lonely man who was expecting me to 'partner' him for the evening at the Hyde Park Hotel! My aunt had gone out. We introduced ourselves feeling rather embarrassed and I discovered he was Australian — the first I had met. Fortunately he was a good dancer and we got on quite well.

The Hyde Park Hotel used to have two large ballrooms with a wide communicating passage where the band played. I was walking through this passage talking to my Australian partner who was slightly behind and as I turned round I just avoided colliding with Edward, Prince of Wales (later Duke of Windsor). Then he spotted my partner and I turned back to see them talking together. When my partner (I have no idea of his name) joined me again he said "That is absolutely amazing — I spoke to His Royal Highness briefly when he was visiting the army in France during the war, and he remembered me after all this time".

In 1926 there was the general strike in England. The coal miners were, quite rightly, asking for safety in the mines, economic security, and decent living conditions. The miners were joined by railway men and transport, building, engineering and printing, which meant newspapers disappeared for the nine-day duration of the strike. We were young in those days and the important issues did not loom very large. The public was with the Government but without resentment against the strikers. It was all rather a lark to those not on strike. University students volunteered for bus and train driving with notices such as "This bus goes anywhere you like. No fares and kind treatment!" Debutantes ran canteens and society women were 'newsboys' or switchboard operators. Motorists gave people lifts to work. I used to start walking from Lancaster Gate to Harley Street but I seldom had to walk very far before some kind soul picked me up. My brother joined the Special Constabulary and was issued with a very nice blue overcoat and a truncheon — the latter I used after the strike when I went on long trips by myself in the car, it fitted nicely into the door-pocket. It was really wonderful how all the essential services were kept going. It is said that 14 years later it brought out in the public, what was to be known as the 'Dunkirk Spirit', a spirit I hope we never lose. Except for the army guarding key danger points, and a few 'incidents', it was incredibly peaceful with many of the 'wheels turning' as usual by the help of willing volunteers.

About this time my father decided to give up his job with the Lifeboat Institution and felt he could branch out on his own with the experience he had gained during the war running hotels commandeered by the army in the north of England. The hotel project was not a success financially and eventually became too much for my parents while the lack of discipline in the guests frustrated my father. The hotel episode cured me of wanting to have anything to do with catering or accommodation for people. The only advantage was that in a round-about way it was through the hotel I met my future husband Christopher Briggs.

An aunt and uncle of Christopher's (Corrie and Kelly Purnell) lived quite close to the hotel and she came to book a room for her brother Godfrey who was up from Wales.

It was some time before I saw Christopher in anything but a dinner-jacket as we went to many dances together while he was in London studying for the first of his three Merchant Service Officer's Certificates, namely 2nd Mate.

Christopher had spent two years on H.M.S. 'Conway', a school-ship anchored in the river Mersey off Rockferry. These two years counted as one year's seatime and he only had to do three years as an apprentice in a merchant ship to enable him to qualify for the Board of Trade examinations. As was the custom in those days his father had been required to pay a premium of £50 to have him apprenticed to the Ellerman Hall Line of Liverpool. This was repaid in the form of wages at the 'princely' rate of £1 per month the first year, £2 per month the second year, and £4 per month the third year. They provided him with food and laundry when the ship was in port, but uniform and working clothes had to be supplied by the apprentice.

After my first meeting with Christopher we saw a great deal of each other whenever he was not at sea. We thought it was a good idea but our families did not, and those two years were not always the easiest. I wish I still had some of the interesting letters written by Christopher from various ports of the world, especially one that was 21 pages — which was quite a record!

One weekend before we were married we went to stay with my grandmother Harden at Colchester. We decided to go to a dance about 10 miles away and whilst travelling on his motorbike through a small village we hit a black dog which ran across the road in front of a stationary bus. Fortunately we were travelling very slowly and as we hit the dog I slid gracefully backwards off the pillion — the dog was not hurt and Christopher extricated himself from the motorbike. His overcoat was slightly torn and the shoes inside his pocket had bruised his rib. It was not until many years later, when he joined the Navy on 1st November, 1939, that the examining naval doctor said to him, ''When did you break that rib?''!

My mother was always extremely worried until we got safely home from our motorbike expeditions. One certainly felt very vulnerable sitting on a pillion going through London even in those days, with great two-decker buses towering above. I used to hope the drivers knew we were there!

Christopher's mother before her marriage was Beatrice (Budge) Vaughan, and her home was at Layfield, Millom, Cumberland. This lovely old house is now deserted and dilapidated. It had been the managing director's house owned by the Hodbarrow Mining Company, which her father, Cedric Vaughan, founded in 1855. This mine produced a very high-grade haematite ore which was easily transported by sea as the mine was situated on the estuary of the Duddon River. In 1968 the Hodbarrow mine finally closed down after some 100 years of operation, during which time 25 million tons of ore were raised. A peak annual production of 538,373 was reached in 1894 and production for the last year was only 20,955 tons. This was, of course, an underground mine and some of the mining took place under the sea but with a sea wall, or barrier, keeping the sea out from over the mine. A complete history of this unique mine is given in a book entitled 'Cumberland Iron' by H. Harris.

Christopher's mother came from a large family of four boys and five girls. She was an excellent horsewoman. Her eldest sister, Ethel, became the Harley Street gynaecologist as mentioned earlier and during her medical training she must have introduced medical students into the family with the result that one of her sisters married a doctor and two of her brothers married women doctors, quite an achieve-

7th Jan. 1930. Author being escorted by her father to Holy Trinity, Brompton.

ment at the turn of the century when there were few women doctors. One brother went into the navy and another, General Sir Louis Vaughan, was G.O.C. in India at one time.

Christopher's mother married Philip L. Briggs on November 16th 1898, and after losing four babies — two in Canada and twins at Millom — Christopher was born at Cowes, Isle-of-Wight, with her brother-in-law in attendance and in their house.

The Briggs' were originally Lancashire cotton-spinners from Bolton. They had been wealthy but the grandfather died suddenly during one of the 'flu epidemics' and at a point when his finances were at a low ebb. His widow moved to Herefordshire with the two youngest children — Cordelia and Godfrey — and Philip was at that time at the Royal Military College, Sandhurst — much against his will. So on the death of his father he left Sandhurst and went to Canada — taking with him the first pack of English foxhounds in about 1899, some of them from the well-known kennels at 'Goggerdan', Wales.

He took a small place on the Bow River at Calgary and started breeding and riding his own racehorses — in Canada in the summer and the United States in the winter. The foxhounds were used for hunting coyote on the prairie, and the mounted head of one of these was still in his house when he died in 1947, but unfortunately we had to leave it behind when later we came to Australia.

The cold of Canada and living in hard conditions was too much for my poor mother-in-law and after losing two of her babies they returned to Britain. Having sufficient income to live on my father-in-law never returned to his horse-breeding activities, but went to live where the fishing and shooting was good — the west of Ireland and later Wales.

On the 7th January, 1930 our wedding took place at the beautiful church of Holy Trinity, Brompton — and the sun actually shone for a few minutes — quite an achievement for London in January. We were married by the popular and dynamic Prebendary Gough. Holy Trinity is a large and lovely church and at Sunday morning service it was always full with extra seats having been added on each side of the exceptionally wide aisle. It was a small wedding, mostly family and a few friends and schoolmates, not nearly big enough for Holy Trinity, Brompton, and I felt very lonely walking up the aisle on my father's arm.

Our wedding reception was given by my grandmother Harden's sister Jeanie (Mrs. Pat Osborne of Currandooley, N.S.W.). Her home in Ennismore Gardens was close to the church. She had married Pat Hill

Osborne at the age of 18 and returned with him to Australia. Curran-dooley, on the shores of Lake George, was built for her after they were flooded out of a house nearer the lake. There is still a Pat Osborne living there today. She returned to England for the education of her 10 children, remaining there after the death of her husband and lived in London where her family and many Australians were always made welcome. She used to go regularly to the Star and Garter home at Richmond where she visited the maimed and limbless men from World War I. Holy Trinity, Brompton was her parish church and she wanted the wedding to be there.

I am glad to say that my family were marvelous when the time came and Christopher's mother, who had very bad eyesight, came all the way from Wales for the wedding. It was sadly many years before his father accepted me as a daughter-in-law which he did, in a touching way just before he died. I was grateful but sad it had not happened long before.

My brother Bill was our best-man and looked very smart in his top hat and morning suit. We had a large square wedding cake made by 'Buzzard's' of Oxford Street, with two white anchors on the top — carefully treasured by my mother — and later to adorn our golden wedding cake in Australia!

After the service Christopher gave his wallet to Bill to pay for any expenses and off we drove in my aunt's car. It was not until we were driving through Kensington Gardens that we realized we had no money — Christopher had forgotten to collect the wallet! So there we were, launched into married life without any money, and that problem has continued in varying degrees ever since. We sat on a seat in Kensington Gardens while the chauffeur returned to retrieve the money and enable us to continue on our way. After a short honeymoon in Bournemouth — bleak and deserted in January — Christopher went to sea for six months and I returned to my job.

I remember so well travelling to Portsmouth to meet Christopher on his return. I stayed at the old Keppels Head Hotel to be handy to the naval dockyard. Next morning a note was brought to my room from the captain's wife, who unknown to me was staying at the same hotel. She invited me to go out with her to the ship which was anchored outside the harbour waiting for the pilot. This seemed absolutely marvellous and very unexpected. It was a new experience to sail into harbour on the high bridge of an admiralty oil tanker and I remember it was such a beautiful sunny day, with Portsmouth sparkling in the distance. I took some snaps but in my excitement I took 2 or 3 on the same negative!

Christopher had bought our first car, a 1923 two-seater Swift No. TP251 for the large sum of £11. After many long trips and my learning to drive on it we sold it for £9 — not a bad transaction! I can not remember the number of our present car, but I will never forget that one. We drove up to London from Portsmouth and I little knew at the time that it was the first car Christopher had driven — before it had only been motorbikes! We then had a spell in London while he sat for his master's certificate and I kept my job.

Our first 'home' was a bedsitter at Swiss Cottage where we lived while he was studying.

When Christopher went to sea again and I had given up my job, I decided to try and add to our income by making bright-coloured men's pymamas. I had cards printed advertising "Briggs' Brighter Bedwear" which I distributed to all my friends. I do not think my in-laws approved of the venture. The business commenced well until my mother became ill with pneumonia. In those days there were no antibiotic drugs so the illness was prolonged and the recovery slow. It was most fortunate that I was completely free to nurse her.

My brother and I had decided to share 'TP251' while Christopher was at sea. I had not yet driven solo, but after a while I realized that the arrangement with Bill was turning out rather one-sided and that all I needed was the courage to take the plunge. I had a friend living in Kensington whom I wanted to see, and I was living with my parents near Harrow at that time. It was a beautiful morning when I left home and I had a great feeling of enjoyment and achievement in venturing forth on my first solo drive. I turned into High Street, Kensington, but unfortunately the policeman stopped the traffic at the bottom of Church Street — I then stalled my engine. This meant getting out to swing the handle (no self-starter in this car!) but the noise of the traffic was so great that I had to put my head inside the car to hear if the engine had started! All this happened with the traffic and double-deckers surging round me. By this time I was really jittery and was determined not to stall the engine again so shot up Church Street grating my gears, the policeman and everyone turning to stare.

I arrived safely at Aunt Corrie's but feeling too shaky to really enjoy my lunch. This baptism into the traffic of a great city stood me in good stead for the rest of my life and traffic has never worried me since, in fact I find it more interesting from a driving point of view than the open road.

52

We had many happy trips driving TP251 and many memorable experiences.

Our longest trips were usually between London and Wales, and our first trip to Wales was in the middle of winter. It was bitterly cold in a small open car chugging along the road over Plynlimon (a climb of over 2000 ft. in the Welsh mountains) when we developed engine trouble. This meant pulling into the side of the deserted road, taking all our belongings out of the boot to get at the tools and laying our things on the snow-covered bank.

It was a while before Christopher was appointed to another ship as it was the beginning of the depression, so we had a spell staying with his parents in Wales while we waited hopefully. We were very apprehensive about the job situation but joined in the life around us and I got to know a part of Wales and its people. It was quiet and peaceful; we walked — played golf — and turned up at the 'meets' of the local foxhounds, and visited some of the old Welsh families, one being the very large and beautiful old house called 'Goggerdan' that had belonged to the Pryse family for many years. The hunt-ball was always held at Goggerdan and was a great occasion in the countryside. Christopher's uncle Godfrey had married into the Pryse family, so it was also rather a family affair. Old Sir Lew Pryse was a widower and lived there alone. He did most of the cooking for the ball himself and I remember a whole sucking-pig in aspic beautifully cooked and decorated by him.

The night we went to the hunt-ball was bitterly cold and the fun started when we were all rugged-up in our small open car ready to drive 20 miles home to Aberayron. The car would not start. This meant kettles of boiling water and much pushing and advice from guests!! It was a cold drive back but we had thoroughly enjoyed ourselves. I understand 'Goggerdan' is now an agricultural college and part of the University of Aberystwyth and known all over the world for the agricultural research that has been carried out there over many years.

Eventually a job turned up for Christopher and he went to sea for another six months. When he returned his next appointment was to Portland, Dorset, near Weymouth. We rented a small bungalow at Wyke Regis and were able to have my family for our first Christmas together since we were married. Towns in Britain with 'Regis' after the name shows that at some time a reigning monarch has stayed in that place, but this habit seems to have been dropped. Wyke Regis is connected to Portland by the famous Chesil Beach — unique in the world, a long stretch of some ten miles of beach consisting of large smooth round stones and a graveyard of many sailing ships.

In Weymouth Christopher was chief officer on the base oiler at Portland, R.F.A. 'Scotol'. It was a pleasant job and he came home every night instead of being months at sea. However, this was not to last, because soon after Christmas we received word from the admiralty that he was appointed for three years to the base oiler in Hong Kong. He had to go back to second officer and sail on a P. & O. ship in mid-January 1932. Jobs were virtually unobtainable, as the whole world was at the height of the great depression and to refuse to go would have been a very difficult decision.

If he had refused the Hong Kong posting, we might have been in very serious trouble facing complete unemployment. There really was no choice and there was no prospect of my being able to afford to join him in Hong Kong. I did not want to start another job so we decided to start a family instead. I did not weigh the pro's and con's as they do these days as to whether we could afford it or not, but felt it would be marvellous and that everything would turn out all right.

Chapter 3

CHINA 1933-1937

Soon after arriving in China, Christopher met my cousin Douglas (D.B.W. Murray), who was in the Chinese Maritime Customs. At that time the customs were needing men with masters certificates for their launches and ships of the Marine Department. This meant good pay and conditions and the prospect of my being able to join him later. The problem was to repay to Admiralty the equivalent of Christopher's fare to China and his pay during the voyage. Though this was only £72 it was the sort of sum we did not have. We tried Christopher's father, but he was quite adamant that Christopher should not leave the oil tanker and would not help. It cost me many phone calls to Wales trying to explain but with no luck. Eventually, my mother came to the rescue. There was no time to lose as there was a customs ship in Hong Kong and they wanted him to take passage on it to Shanghai (the custom's headquarters) immediately. This new job meant everything to us for the future and was in fact the turning-point in our lives.

This book would not be complete without some further description of the maritime customs of China — a unique organisation — the like of which will never be seen again.

China's desire to borrow money from the foreign powers and also the need to pay reparations for certain 'incidents' saw the conclusion of the treaties of Tientsin in 1859. Under this treaty between China and Great Britain, the U.S.A. and Russia, an Imperial Maritime Customs was established with a foreign general inspector, one Horatio N. Lay. The word 'maritime' is used to differentiate this customs from the internal customs barriers between various provinces.

In 1863, Sir Robert Hart, an Irishman, was appointed as inspector-general and during the years to 1908 built up the customs into a magnificent and far-reaching service. His instructions from the Chinese government were to train men — light the coast — improve rivers and harbours — and organize a postal service. The last became independent in 1911.

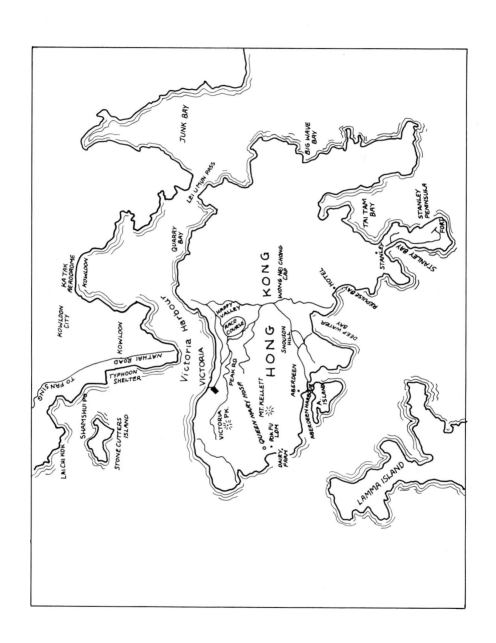

JUNK BAY

BIG WAVE BAY

LEI U MUN PASS

STANLEY PENINSULA

QUARRY BAY

TAI TAM BAY

FORT

KA TAK AERODROME

KOWLOON

STANLEY

STANLEY BAY

HONG KONG

WONG NEI CHONG GAP

KOWLOON CITY

KOWLOON

REPULSE BAY HOTEL

DEEP WATER BAY

Victoria Harbour

HAPPY VALLEY

RACE COURSE

VICTORIA

NATHAI ROAD

TYPHOON SHELTER

TO FAN LING

PEAK RD

MT. KELLETT

HONG KONG

SNOUSON HILL

SHAMSHUI PO

VICTORIA PK.

QUEEN MARY HOSP.

POK FU LOM

ABERDEEN

A. ISLAND

ABERDEEN HARBOUR

LAI CHI KOK

STONE CUTTERS ISLAND

DAIRY FARM

LAMMA ISLAND

By 1875 Hart headed a foreign staff of 252 from Britain and 156 from 16 other western countries, with of course, many hundreds of Chinese clerks, examiners, tidewaiters, boatmen etc.

In 1898 Britain secured an agreement from China to open her inland waterways to foreign trade and in addition, that a Briton should hold the post of inspector general of customs as long as Britain held the majority of the trade.

After the Chinese revolution in 1911 when the Manchu dynasty was overthrown, the word 'Imperial' was dropped and it became the Chinese Maritime Customs. At this time the inspector general was responsible for the servicing and repayment of foreign loans, the payment of the various indemnities which had been extracted from China by the powers. Any surplus revenue, after these payments were made, was handed over to the Chinese government of the time.

In addition to the revenue collecting departments there was a large marine department, the staffing of which was predominantly British, Scandinavian and Danish.

By this time the customs was responsible for the building and maintenance of all the lighthouses on the China coast, the pilotage of the rivers and harbours, the maintenance of minor navigational aids, including buoyage. At Shanghai there was a spacious and well-equipped buoy yard at Pootung across the river. In the customs house on the Bund, where the marine department was housed, there was an up-to-date chart and survey department.

With the opening to foreign trade of the inland waterways the customs was faced with the massive task of erecting and maintaining navigational aids for the Yangtze River. The Yangtze is navigable for ocean going vessels as far as Hankow, some 800 miles from the sea, and some 4-500 miles further up for specially constructed craft.

Towards the end of the 1920s, when General Chiang Kai Shek came to power and the government of China became stabilized with the Kuomintang government, the powers agreed to allow China to have tariff autonomy. This meant that the customs could now be used to raise revenue for the government and the responsibility of servicing foreign loans was no longer that of the I.G. of customs. This led China to impose a wide range of high tariffs on all imported goods, this in its turn leading to an immediate increase of smuggling from such places as Korea, Formosa, Hong Kong, Macao and French Indo-China. So it was then decided to build up a sea-going 'preventative force' of small armed patrol vessels. This meant recruiting foreign sea-going officers to man these vessels, as there were insufficient qualified Chinese available as officers at that time. The crews, were however, no problem.

It was at this point in 1932 that Christopher joined the service and we began some of the happiest times of our life together.

On the 8th October 1932 our daughter Patricia was born. She was born in the home of my parents near Harrow and I was fortunate in being able to really look after her without all the interruptions of running a house. My only sadness was that she was to be a year old before her father saw her. She was everything a mother could wish for, healthy, happy and beautiful, and a great joy to me and to all the family. Patricia and I left England in September 1933 on the P. & O. *S.S. 'Comorin'* and she had her first birthday at sea off Bombay.

I had considered going by 'cargo' ship, as the fare was considerably cheaper, but I was not sure how well I would be at sea, and having a baby to care for, it was too much of a risk — a very fortunate decision as it turned out as I was such a bad sailor. I answered an advertisement in the *'Morning Post'* from a naval officer's wife going to join her husband in *H.M.S. Kent* on the China station, and willing to help with children on the voyage. Her name was Mollie Webb, and I wrote to her really to make a friendly contact for the voyage, explaining that I could not afford to help her financially. She was very nice and as she'd no other answers to her advertisement we made friends and she kindly offered to give me a hand if necessary. In the end we discovered that she was only a few hours each way less seasick than I was — she went down later than I and got up a bit before me! The ship had a fancy-dress dance that we both wanted to go to and hearing that champagne was a great help for seasickness we decided to split a small bottle. She joined in the festivities — but not I!

It was not easy trying to look after a one-year-old baby when it was impossible to get off my bunk for more than a few minutes at a time. The purser's office put a notice on the board for help and an extremely nice missionary girl came to the rescue for which I was most grateful, but unfortunately she did not seem to know the simplest rudiments of 'nappy' changing. I felt sorry for her going into the interior of China with so little common knowledge.

My brother Bill met the ship at Bombay and took us for a drive up Malabar Hill at 6 a.m. It was marvellous to see him and he was delightful with Patricia, their first meeting. I loved all the places we called at, first Colombo where my cousin Kenneth Murray and his family met us and took us home to dinner, then Penang where we were met by friends of Christopher's family called Winter of the Hong Kong and Shanghai bank. They took us home for the day to their

The Harbour of Hong Kong 1934-35. The Star Ferry terminal centre foreground and Victoria Peak (561m) rising above the city of Victoria.

lovely house where I had my first experience of a deep and luxurious bath in a Chinese 'kong'. A 'kong' is a glazed earthenware tub which is filled by hand, big enough to sit down and deep enough for the water to come right up to your shoulders. Cool air from the 'punkah' over the dining-room table was the first I experienced. The 'punkah' was pulled by a 'chi tsai' (small boy) who sat outside the room and pulled the cord, often attached to his toe.

Our next port of call was Singapore, where we were met by Major and Mrs. Foster-Hall. Later we met his brother Dick in the Chinese Maritime Customs. Their children had unfortunately developed impetigo which made our day difficult as it is so contagious, but they were very kind to us and it was wonderful to be off the ship.

Eventually we arrived in Hong Kong to be met by two complete strangers, Jim and Iris Skinner, who were later in life to meet me from a ship on two momentuous and traumatic occasions. Christopher had unfortunately been delayed 24 hours in Shanghai but arrived the next day.

The Skinners were both so kind to us and helped to settle us into our room in Gloucester Building, then in Pedder Street.

What a fascinating and dreamlike place to me, all the sights and sounds and smells drifting up to my room on the top floor. That night I stood on my balcony and it seemed I was up with the stars, then I turned, saw the shadow of the Peak towering up behind me with the lights of the houses leading up into the sky and wished Christopher was standing beside me to enjoy it with me. My first morning in Hong Kong I woke to an unusual and incessant noise. Later I discovered the sound was the clip-clop of wooden clogs on the pavement far below. I always feel 'at home' when I hear anything resembling that familiar sound.

The name Hong Kong literally means 'Fragrant Harbour'. The capital is Victoria, named after Queen Victoria. When the British sailors first arrived in the early 1800s, they used the fishing village of Aberdeen as a watering place. Aberdeen is a harbour in its own right on the opposite side of the island to Victoria and the site of the original Hong Kong. There is a rocky stream there that discharges into the harbour and the village was called Huen Kong Wai, which means 'The Walled Village of the Fragrant Lagoon'. The sailors learnt the Chinese name and pronounced it Hong Kong, which in effect became Hong Kong the colony and the city, and today that is what nearly everyone, Chinese and British, call it.

The island of Hong Kong is separated from the mainland of China by a very beautiful natural harbour. Its views are superb, one of the most beautiful places in the world. Just as the light is fading one can still see the outline of land and sea with the lights of the many ships in the harbour or the houses dotted up the Peak, it is truly a picture that lingers in one's memory. The distance from mainland to island at the narrowest point is one mile across and was crossed by passenger ferry, car ferry or sampan (now I hear there is a tunnel under the harbour!). The tip of the mainland known as Kowloon (or Nine Dragons) is land leased to the British and extends inland for about 20 miles. The drive round the New Territories, as it is called, is roughly 52 miles, and is the longest drive that one can take. It was very pleasant to drive through the pretty country side and villages, with their lush green paddy fields and slow moving waterbuffalos. One passed through Tai Po (where later the hoards of Japanese came through on their way to Hong Kong) and through Fanling where we used to play golf. Hong Kong island is only nine miles long and 6 miles at its widest point. The drive round was 15 miles, a drive we used to enjoy on a hot summer night.

Before the war the population was about 2 million, but dropped to 500,000 during the Japanese occupation. It consisted of Chinese, English, Indian, Japanese, American, Portugese and many other nationalities.

One soon got used to the harsh language of the luggage and rickshaw coolies, but the hawking and spitting — known to us foreigners as the 'Chinese Anthem' took longer to get used to.

Christopher arrived from Shanghai next morning and it was strange to see how terrified he appeared of his little daughter at first.

There were many readjustments to make after 1½ years separation - a house and servants to find — and a very new life to get used to. One was expected to have a minimum staff of a Cook-boy, House-boy, Baby-amah, and Wash-amah. Larger households would perhaps have two or more of each, also perhaps a gardener and rickshaw-coolie. I understand that today one would need to be very wealthy to be able to afford even the modest staff that we had, which varied slightly according to the house we were in.

It was almost unbelievable to me that I was really in Hong Kong with Christopher. I loved the gay life and friends which was something I had always missed — the friends we made were also part of our job and we had many interests together. I had to master the speaking of 'Pidgin-English'. At first I found it very difficult to make myself understood — and the fact that there seemed to be no words such as 'yes' or 'no' only 'I think so can do' or 'I think so no can do' made for a certain amount of frustration until I got used to it. 'Pidgin-English' is quite different to 'Pidgin' of Papua New Guinea, 'Pidgin-English' is the translation of the literal Chinese expressions. The Chinese language has no 'R' in the alphabet — it is always pronounced 'L' — hence 'Briggs' becomes 'Bliggs' or 'very pretty' becomes 'Velly pletty' or again 'that man is making a lot of trouble' becomes 'that man make plenty tlouble — he no good!' After one speaks that way for a time it almost becomes a second language.

We had various homes in the two years we were in Hong Kong, due to the fact that the usual method of renting European houses was to take one from someone who was going on 'leave' for six months. Two of these houses we particularly liked. The first was a delightful bungalow overlooking the Happy Valley racecourse, where later so many dreadful things happened when the Japanese landed. It was really a two-storey building — we lived on the first floor and my kitchen and the staff quarters were underneath. Every time I went to the kitchen to arrange the menu I was confronted by a strange face, and on asking "Who man he belong?" was told "He belong Boy's brother" or "Amah's son" as the case might be. This went on for quite a while, until one night after we had been out to dinner with friends further up the private road, we were walking back and saw a Chinese man go to one of the downstairs windows which were grilled, put his hand through, take a key and let himself in. We followed — woke everybody up and 'read the riot act', and discovered that for sometime we had been giving free lodging to any of their friends who needed a bed. Hence all the strange faces I used to see around.

The first thing that happened in a series of strange events was that Christopher was promoted Captain of one of the senior customs cruisers, the 'Likin'. I can remember so vividly taking him down to join the ship and sitting having tea in his delightful quarters, but somehow quite suddenly, we were both very quiet and sad. It seemed as if something was ending — neither of us referred to it until long afterwards. He sailed, and I went home to Patricia. That evening I began to feel very ill and during the night I became worse. Amah called the doctor and he told me I had bacillary dysentery and must go at once to hospital. He arranged for an ambulance to take me over to the Canossa Hospital on the first ferry at daylight. I was very worried leaving Patricia but hoped it was only for a few days — I was in hospital five weeks. As soon as word got round in the customs, a family called Everest with two little girls of Patricia's age collected her and her Amah, and took them to their home up the Peak and cared for her there — all this unbeknown to me as I was very ill by this time, but what a great relief when I heard, and a wonderful gesture on their part. Eventually Christopher returned from a long trip to Hainan Island to find me nearly at the end of my tether — in fact, he was called at daybreak next morning to come and say 'goodbye'. I was aware of his presence and of vaguely hearing the harbour ferry but of little else and had no idea of the early hour. I had been given all the drug available in Hong Kong and there was little hope, but happily I began to rally from that point and Christopher was able to take me to the Happy Valley bungalow where he had moved while I was in hospital.

What was that strange, sad feeling trying to tell us the afternoon he sailed?

The bungalow was a lovely quiet place to rest and recuperate. My nerves were bad for sometime after my illness and I felt nervous when Christopher was away, so for a while I slept with a revolver under my pillow — terrified I would forget to put it in the safe before the 'House Boy' made my bed! It was a heavy sort of firearm and I would probably have done more damage than good had I tried to use it but it made me feel safer.

The second tragedy while Christopher was in command of the 'Likin' was when, on patrol one night in Chinese waters outside Hong Kong, they collided with a large fishing junk with an unfortunate loss of life. This was a terrible thing to have happened and, as you can imagine, needed a lot of explanation at the subsequent inquiry. The third tragedy for us was when Christopher was leaving the ship on transfer to Shanghai; one of his officers superintending the steward packing up his belongings was asked by the steward if the pistol belonged to Christopher or to the ship? The officer said that it belonged to Christopher then picked it up — pushed the magazine home and shot himself through the hand. Fortunately it was a clean wound and no broken bones.

We heard later that the 'Likin' was known as an unlucky ship for some of her captains — strange but true — as a great friend of ours Capt. Ian MacRoberts who later took command of her, had the tragic experience of losing his wife — something that so nearly happened to me.

When I was stronger, Patricia and I were invited to go to Hainan Island to stay with Commissioner and Mrs. 'Bingo' Joly. Hainan Island is in the South China Sea, near what was French Indo-China. A small tip of the mainland opposite Hainan called Quanshowan was French territory and it was from there they used to smuggle across to Hainan, hence there was a customs station at Hoihow on the island. It was about 400 miles from Hong Kong, so we spent one night on board. We took on a load of Chinese pigs and if you have ever travelled with the poor things you will understand how very unpleasant they are. The smell is overpowering and the squealing in spite of the drugging is constant. Coming back we took on board a load of the delicious lichee fruit. This in bulk has a most unpleasant smell, but an improvement on the pigs, and we survived.

We loved our short stay with the Joly's — and as it was high tide when we arrived they did not have to carry me ashore, much to their relief. Swimming in the warm sea was very pleasant, playing plenty of tennis, and enjoying the balmy evenings. I also enjoyed the experience of being taken on target practice with the Chinese customs guards. I am afraid I did not excel with a revolver but it was good fun. It was a short but memorable experience in a small customs outpost and the Joly's were very kind hosts.

Christopher's next ship was being built in Shanghai and the three of us sailed north in a coaster. He had to be with the new ship while she was fitting-out and for trials. The ship was called the *'Soohsing'* and was a shallow draft ship specially designed to work in the Canton delta. It was a chance for me to get to know Shanghai and the people, and to meet my cousin Douglas Murray whom I had not seen for about twelve years. It was my first taste of really hot weather, but we enjoyed our short time there, and everyone was very kind to us. When the *'Soohsing'* was ready to sail we returned to Hong Kong.

Our next home was a lovely spot above the Pokfulam Road, looking out to sea with Lamma Island in the distance. There were three large houses belonging to Mrs. Weill senior, whose family owned the well-known Hong Kong jewellers Sennet Freres. She lived in one house and her son Leo (later to die in a Japanese prison camp) lived in another. The third house she had divided into two flats. We had the top flat, with a lovely view towards Lantau Island, and three German bachelors had the ground floor. There was a tennis court where Patricia and other children used to play with Leo's two sons, about her own age. How wonderfully peaceful at night to sit on the verandah watching the Chinese boats with their bright lights fishing away out to sea.

At this time we acquired two liver-and-white pointers, 'Sue' and 'Nigger', both very beautiful and very affectionate. Sometimes they were both at home but usually they alternately went to sea with Christopher. One night we came home from a party and let Sue out

1935 Hong Kong. C.P.S. Soohsing — 'Dressed Ship'.

1934 Hong Kong. Christopher with Nigger and Sue on board C.P.S. Kuanlui.

and she raced across the tennis court barking madly. We called but she refused to come, eventually we got angry and brought her in. Next morning there was consternation from the Germans below — long bamboo poles had been pushed through the grills over their window and their trousers and wallets had been hooked out! This taught us never to ignore a dog barking until one was sure what they were barking about. The thieves had obviously been hiding in the bushes.

The dogs both enjoyed their trips to sea and at the right time of the year Christopher took them shooting in the Chinese countryside. There were pigeons, quail, wild duck and snipe, and the country people were very friendly. Nigger particularly loved being towed on a board with Christopher behind one of the motor-boats — this was before the days of fast boats and water-skis.

Eventually our living in Hong Kong came to an end and we were transferred to Shanghai. We found a nice house and garden belonging to tramway staff who were away on leave. We loved our year in Shanghai — known as the 'Paris of the East' — very hot in summer, cold and wet in winter, smelly and dirty, but a wonderfully friendly, gay, and cosmopolitan place. We were there from October 1935 to October 1936, and met Americans, White Russians, Scandinavians, and many others, some of whom were customs staff. We played a lot of tennis and danced a lot, on dance floors on the roof tops of some of the clubs, and even in the excessive heat it seemed cool up there. There were many bridge parties and the hostesses always had a Mah Jong table at which I played. One favourite house was the lovely home of Mr. and Mrs. Barentzen. She was Eurasian and he was Danish. He was head of one of the customs departments and was a very senior person. Mrs. Barentzen was an outstanding Shanghai personality and hostess and was always very smart. She used to say "My mother was a sampan woman and my father was a Lord". Maybe her story was a little exaggerated but basically it was true. She was stone deaf — she played bridge, danced and went shooting and was the only one in the party who was able to ride on a water buffalo — as she was partly Asian it accepted her. A water buffalo will not accept white people because they smell too strong. White people find this hard to understand and think that it is the reverse but when we were home on leave in 1938, we went to the second performance of a cinema one evening and when the doors opened and the crowd came out and we went in I did not know how I could stand the smell which was literally sickening. We had been living in North China for fifteen months and out of contact with European crowds.

Since then I have always been sorry for coloured people who have to put up with our smugness about ourselves and our criticisms of them. It is not a matter of cleanliness — it is because we eat so much more meat.

The inspector general of the Chinese customs and his wife, when we were in Shanghai, were Sir Frederick and Lady Maze. She was a descendant of the famous Captain Bligh, of *H.M.S. Bounty* and came from Australia. It was from her that I learned to make my Christmas puddings a year in advance and have done so ever since. They mature and are delicious.

One day a German doctor came to see Patricia as she was not well. When he arrived, the key to the strong five-foot wooden gate could not be found. It was an embarrassing situation, with a busy doctor locked outside. However, he decided to climb over and was teetering on the top to jump down when 'Nigger' spotted him and it was touch and go which way the doctor would jump until someone rescued him! It was a strange sight I have never forgotten — but all ended well, Patricia had nothing serious, and the key was found in time to let the doctor out by the gate.

In Hong Kong I had been used to doing quite a lot of my household shopping and paying directly for it, but in Shanghai I was to learn differently. My nice house-boy came to me in great distress one day as I had paid the household bills. He explained to me that he needed to pay the bills as he was entitled to 'cumshaw' (gratuity) on the amount of the account. You either accepted this custom or you lost your house-boy. There was no dishonesty about this — it was openly accepted.

All the time I was in China I found the Chinese very honest. I never needed to lock my valuables away and I never lost anything. A bit of 'squeeze' or to bargain relentlessly was a different thing altogether. If you did not bargain, the sale had not been much fun and you were considered to be a bit of a fool anyway.

One day we came home to find our kitchen a hive of activity with every burner on our electric stove in full use. It turned out that the cook's brother owned a mobile food stall and our kitchen was used to keep it going! These food stalls consist of two large baskets containing the food and the utensils, and are carried on a bamboo pole over the shoulder. You set up on the pavement in some busy place and you are in business. Normally all the staff do their cooking on the Chinese 'Chatti', which is a small brick stove using charcoal.

Unfortunately, I had to go to hospital at that time for an operation. One day when Christopher got home after visiting me, 'Nigger'

Shanghai 1936. Christopher, Patricia and Nigger having difficulty to sit after injections!

Shanghai 1936. Patricia in our garden.

could not be found anywhere and he got very angry with the house-boy for letting him disappear. Patricia used to love dressing him up in her baby clothes, complete with bonnet, and he joined in the fun, strutting round, pleased as punch with himself and wagging his tail. What really happened was not clear, but off our bedroom was a large walk-in wardrobe, and 'Nigger' had walked in with Patricia, was left behind for some reason and shut in. It was the last place anyone thought of looking. When Christopher opened the door to put his clothes away, out came 'Nigger' still dressed up and wagging his tail.

Another day we took 'Nigger' in the car to a delightful place where we could have a walk along the paddy fields outside Shanghai and he nearly caused what could have become an 'international incident'. It was all very pleasant and peaceful with not a soul in sight, then suddenly the peace was shattered — yells and barks and people all round us, it was amazing where they all sprang from. One man with a fur hat grabbed Christopher by the lapel of his coat and they all started shouting and screaming at us and although we could not speak Chinese we understood quite clearly that our dog had damaged their tethered goat. It was not a very pleasant situation, miles from anywhere, but we were fortunate enough to see another European couple — also out for a walk — coming along the paddy fields. They spoke fluent Chinese and were able to sort things out and find what the actual damage to the goat was. It turned out to be a nip on one of its hooves. The couple came to our rescue and arranged we should all meet at their house in a week to assess any lasting damage, but the villagers never turned up so we presumed that all was well with the goat.

At the time we left Shanghai 'Nigger' was very sick. He had been bitten on the nose — the only spot free of hair — by a certain mosquito that eventually causes tiny worms in the blood stream. We took him to the vet, who explained that he could give him an injection to kill the worms, but that there was a 50% chance of killing the dog too. However, we took the risk. The worms died but he developed a pheumonia condition and his breathing was very laboured. We were determined to take him with us so made him a pneumonia jacket and sewed him up in that. With careful nursing he recovered completely and was soon his old self — fighting any small dog he saw.

Postings in the customs were always made in October or April and sadly our year in Shanghai and Christopher's year ashore in the customs house came to an end in October 1936. We had made many friends there and some we were to meet again on different occasions and in different places. I was glad for Patricia's sake to be leaving Shanghai as the climate was not good, and it was just a teeming city with only private gardens for her to play in.

We had Japanese to pack all our things and they did a marvellous job. Every item, large or small, was separately wrapped in straw. I had a shock to see my large and heavy cut-glass bowl being thrown from one packer to the next at the other end of the dining-room. Not a thing was broken when we unpacked.

After many hilarious farewells we piled on the S.S. 'Shuntien' of Butterfield and Swire's to take us north to Chefoo in the province of Shantung — very near to where I was born.

On board we received a telegram from our friends addressed to 'Sizzle and Sozzle' which caused a lot of amusement. Even if perhaps it was not quite fair it was quite clever as I was always called 'Sis' and Christopher had a penchant for pink-gins!

Chefoo was a delightful place in summer, with pleasant weather and lots of lovely fruit. The winters are severe and the sea often freezes for three miles out, so Christopher could walk across the harbour to his ship. Walking in the biting wind that blew down from the Gobi Desert made the tears run down your face and freeze on your coat collar.

Most people walked, rode bicycles, or rode in rickshaws. There were only two private cars in Chefoo when we were there; one was owned by the Methodist Mission and the other by Mrs. Silverthorne, a local personality whose father was an English sea-captain and whose mother was Japanese. I played Mah-jong regularly with her in her Chinese-style house on the waterfront, solidly built with some of the beams from her father's ship. She had adopted two Chinese children and later was to befriend the young Japanese soldiers with hot drinks when they came to Chefoo. A very kind and clever woman who at that time owned half Chefoo.

In a large compound facing the sea stood the China Inland Mission School. This unique school came into being in 1881 when the founder of the Mission, Mr. Hudson Taylor, went to Chefoo to convalesce after an illness. He realized it would be a perfect place for a school for children from all over China. The school was to provide teaching in English and to prepare students for tertiary education in Britain, a necessity as schooling for westerners in China was sparse in those days. The Chefoo school progressed and grew, up to the time of the invasion of China by the Japanese in 1937. The compound housed a preparatory school, girls school, boys school, and many other buildings, also playing fields and tennis courts. The latter used to be flooded and frozen over in the winter and the local residents were allowed to skate there. I tried my luck with poor success.

The Chefoo school buildings are now used by the Chinese army, I believe, but other schools have been opened by the Overseas Missionary Fellowship (formerly China Inland Mission) and they have all retained the name of 'Chefoo', and so the 100-year-old vision lives on.

Many years later (and later in this story) we were to meet two men who were small boys at the school during the time we were in Chefoo. How small the world can be!

Our gardener-cum-rickshaw coolie had an unusual method of preserving vegetables during the winter — he dug a deep pit where he stored root vegetables to keep them from freezing — partly covering the pit with sacking — and in a corner of the pit he grew endives. The rose bushes he pruned quite drastically and then built the earth up round them to protect them from frost and we had small mounds of snow adorning our flower bed. The Chinese cottages on the hillside each had a grape vine and they were protected by carefully bringing the branches together and burying them in the ground till the spring, when the mounds of vines and roses were uncovered and the new shoots were ready to open.

The hills of North China were devoid of trees. They had been denuded over the centuries by the Chinese using all available wood, even the roots, for firewood and on our walks we saw them still digging up roots to burn. This explains all the rivers of North China being choked with mud causing the terrible floods and creating deserts. The communist regime took this in hand and I understand there has been a vast programme of re-afforestation.

Patricia and I went on lovely walks with the dogs over the hills in the deep snow of winter, it was dry and crisp and I could wear my Chinese boots without getting damp feet. These boots were made with black velvet tops and very thin strong leather soles — I still have them.

The beaches and climate of Chefoo in summer were perfect. We used to see the elderly Chinese men out on the hills flying their kites or taking their cage-birds for a walk. Everything was peaceful in those days.

I had great hopes at that time of visiting my birthplace Peking. I planned to go with the British consul's wife, while Patricia was to stay with the commissioner of customs in Chefoo, Dick Foster-Hall and his wife, whose daughter Tita was her age. But the Japanese had started

1937 Chefoo. Patricia out for a walk in the snow.

Shanghai 1936. Patricia aged nearly four.

Chefoo. Nigger and Dinah back from a run.

their war with China in the north and it would not have been wise to leave home. Sadly I shall never see my birthplace.

We spent our first Christmas in Chefoo with a family called Strandvig. He was the Danish harbourmaster, an employee of the customs. It was a real Danish Christmas. His two sons were about Patricia's age and the three children were given a drum each which after dinner they beat with much accompanying noise as they marched round the table.

The Strandvigs were replaced by a Norwegian couple. At our next Christmas the wife made delightful 'houses' for all the customs children, from very thin brown biscuits stuck together with jam, complete with chimney, window and door and expertly made.

After lunching with the Norwegian family one day we were sitting over coffee when her son Lars Gustav, aged about eleven, came into the room. He stood in front of his mother, clicked his heels and bowed. She explained to me that it was a Norwegian custom for the son to do this in thanks to his mother for the meal. How refreshing and thoughtful compared to the rough and tumble manners of the present day.

I could get the most beautiful shoes made in Chefoo to match my evening dresses. The shoemaker would come to the house, measure round my foot on a piece of brown paper and make any type of shoe I wanted from a fashion magazine picture. I had a lovely pair of suede brogues made which later in Sydney cost me more to have them resoled than the making, and later still were the only pair of shoes I had for 3½ years in a Japanese prison camp. Christopher had a long leather coat and leather thigh boots made to measure which kept him warm on the bridge of his ship in the sub-zero temperature of the North China winter.

Every so often I would get into my rickshaw and be taken down to the Chinese city to buy dress materials. Sometimes a Chinese man would come to the house selling various things but his selection was limited and the shops had lovely materials to choose from.

One street I went down was past a large Catholic Convent. In the 10ft high wall was a gothic arch with a high arched wooden doorway. On this doorway was fixed a wooden crib about 4ft from the ground. This was to receive babies that families did not want. There was an opening in the door through which the babies would be taken by the nuns to be cared for and of course eventually to work for them.

These babies would be girls as they were considered of little use by a poor family. A boy was quite different and a mouth worth feeding, they were an investment for old age and would be expected to provide and care for their parents when that time came.

Another interesting trip I made was to a hairnet factory. This was run by the Catholic Convent. I was taken into a very large room with long tables stretching from one end of the room to the other. Along each table stood young girls, each with the dummy of a head in front of her and intricately making the hairnets over the dummies. These nets were made of real hair and sold by the gross. I bought two gross to take to England when I went on leave and they cost only $1.20 (Shanghai) per gross, a ridiculously low price even in those days.

Christopher's ship went to sea for a week or more then had four or five days in port. His ship now was one of the larger customs cruisers, the *Huahsing*. In Hong Kong I could see the ship coming in or get a phone call and hop into the car and go and meet it, but in Chefoo there was no car and no phone, so when I heard of a delightful vacant house nicknamed 'Otto's Castle' on the headland overlooking the harbour entrance I thought this would be just the spot to live. Our friend Captain Ian MacRobert told me there had been so many tragedies in that house and that he was unable to stay in it for any length of time because of the reaction it gave him so I very quickly gave up my wonderful plan!

I want to give a special mention to our dear and trusted amah Ah Koi from Shekloong near Canton. She came to us first in Hong Kong as a wash-amah and could speak no English. Later when the baby-amah left I asked her to be baby-amah. This meant promotion, more pay and more prestige. She laughed in her usual attractive way and said she could not take it on as she could not speak enough English. But in the end she did and stayed with us for eight years until we were separated by war. She quickly became fluent at speaking English. She was spotlessly clean in her person, adored Patricia and took great care of her. She came with us to Shanghai, where she felt the heat very much and also the cold. This was her first experience of the washing freezing on the line. She then came on to Chefoo. While there she very much wanted to see her son who had gone to Shanghai from Canton. So in the summer of 1937 she went on the trip. I was fortunate to be offered an elderly Chinese lady to take her place temporarily. She wore a black silk jacket and trousers and had bound feet so was not able to run too fast after Patricia! It was interesting to see her unbinding her feet at night and taking off yards of bandage. This custom had been forbidden for some years. As the binding was done when the child was very small, the bandages had to be retained so

1936 Shanghai. Patricia and Ah Koi.

1937. Chefoo. Our Rickshaw-Coolie with Patricia and her toy rickshaw.

that the grossly deformed feet were able to support the weight of the adult body. Bound feet were supposed to be a sign of superior class.

While Ah Koi was in Shanghai in 1937 the Japanese attacked and captured that city. We were very worried about her but after six weeks, she turned up unexpectedly — not looking at all well but pleased to be back and we were certainly pleased to see her.

It was while we were in Chefoo that there was all the sadness about Edward VIII, his wish to marry a twice-divorced woman, Mrs. Wally Simpson, and his eventual abdication. We had missed meeting Mrs. Simpson as she had left Chefoo before we arrived. At that time she was married to Commander Warfield of the United States Navy. People there said that she had a tremendous personality and was a very dominating character.

Chefoo was the summer port for the United States Navy, and Wei Hai Wei, a short distance south of Chefoo, was the summer port for the British Navy. Both these navies needed to get away from the enervating damp summer heat of their home ports, Manila and Hong Kong respectively. When the navy was not there, Chefoo was a very small place with only about sixty Europeans of various nationalities, and it seemed there was a missionary from every known religious denomination. If the Chinese expected a uniting Christianity it was certainly not there for them to see.

In the summer when the American Navy was in Chefoo, there was an influx of Russian cabaret girls from Shanghai and all the cabarets and bars re-opened. We also had the luxury of a men's barber for the summer months. When Christopher grew a full beard the barber kept it trimmed in summer, but when winter came and I had to trim it I realized how extremely difficult this task was.

Our house was three-storey, which needs a fairly large staff and also there was a large garden. We had a cook-boy, house-boy, Ah Koi (Patricia's amah), a wash-man and a gardener who doubled as a private rickshaw-puller and belonged to the house. Northern Chinese are big-boned, slow-spoken and courteous — more congenial than the slight, highly strung and contentious Cantonese. The women did not work as house servants, hence the wash 'man'. One day in the summer I complained to the cook-boy that the milk was very watery and would he mention this to the milkman. The explanation was simple "Just now too many people, must put water. In winter allight plenty milk"! Obviously, there were not enough cows for the American Navy and the cabaret girls as well as the local residents.

The private road where we lived ran up from the beach road to a main thoroughfare in the hills behind. The Chinese troops were organizing the local residents into digging trenches in the surrounding hills, everything was carried by hand or in carts pulled by small ponies or human beings. It was a continuous stream all day and all night and one wondered just what was going on at that time.

As tension grew we were asked to fly our national flags or to paint them on our roof-tops to avoid being bombed in the case of a Japanese attack on Chefoo. We had a flagpole in the garden and flew the Union Jack so that was easy. I went to the back one day to find a flag with five horizontal stripes fluttering from a downpipe. This flag was that of the puppet government that the Japanese had set up in North China. So we were very much under two flags at that moment and the cook-boy obviously wanted the best of both worlds. He was going to make sure that if the Japanese arrived he was going to be all right!

By this time the place was swarming with Chinese troops. They had built networks of trenches in the hills and concrete pillboxes on the water-front and there were sentries everywhere. The sentries carried their rifles and bayonets horizontally over their shoulders pointing to the back and if they turned quickly as you passed, you ran the risk of being hit in the face. Later when the Japanese troops came they carried their bayonets horizontally through their arms pointing to the front and were equally dangerous!

One morning we woke to find that all the Chinese troops had gone and were replaced by Japanese. There had been no fighting in Chefoo itself, the fighting was outside in the country but the hills around had been bombed by the Japanese continuously. This was the start of a long war for us, 1937-45.

We were now living in Japanese-occupied Chefoo. Christopher was no longer allowed to go out on customs patrol. The Japanese did, however, allow the ship to go and tend the local lighthouses for which, among other things, the Chinese customs were responsible. He had to get permission from the Japanese guardship before he left and they sent a young naval officer with him. It was, however, a very rough trip and the poor young sub-lieutenant was very sick indeed, much to the amusement of the Chinese crew. Much 'face' was lost over that incident and subsequently Christopher was allowed to take the ship alone.

Life at this time for the whole population of Chefoo, both Chinese and foreign, was full of uncertainties and one needed to be very careful what one did. There was no curfew but we did not go out after dark unless absolutely necessary. The Japanese never actually visited our house but this could quite easily have happened as they were the only authority in the area. One evening Christopher was coming home from the ship on his bicycle. He passed a bit close to a Japanese sentry who was facing away from him and who swung round suddenly hitting Christopher across the chest with the flat of his bayonet. It was quite dark and the sentry was a bit puzzled about whom he had stopped. He put his hand up, felt Christopher's beard, decided he was not Chinese and waved him on.

One day I was going home along the sea front in my rickshaw and Christopher was riding his bicycle beside me when we saw a lorry coming towards us filled with Japanese sailors. My rickshaw coolie was very frightened and started to turn back but I felt we were more likely to be fired at if he did this so with my heart in my mouth I persuaded him to go on. As we got nearer, all I could see was (what I thought) the muzzle of a machine gun pointing at us from the top of the cab. I was really frightened till I discovered that all they wanted to do was to take a photograph of us and the 'gun' was in fact a camera! I wonder what happened to the photo of that terrified woman and her rickshaw coolie?

Chefoo was first invaded by the Japanese army who were not very pleasant and we kept well out of their way. Quite soon when it became obvious that there was to be no local resistance the army disappeared and the Japanese Navy took over. The attitude of the navy was quite different and they seemed to want to make a good impression. For instance a lighthouse keeper complained to Christopher that a Japanese destroyer had visited him and the officer had confiscated a home-made radio receiver. However the officer had duly signed the visitor's book with his full name, rank, date and the name of the ship. Christopher reported this to the commissioner of customs — a Japanese — and it was obvious that the report went to the Japanese Admiralty. About two months later the captain of the guardship sent for Christopher and when he went on board he was presented with a cardboard box of assorted radio parts, all that was left of the missing set, and was asked to return it to the lighthouse keeper with the apologies of the Imperial Japanese Navy and to say that the officer had been reprimanded!

Our term in Chefoo was now coming to an end and the customs headquarters in Shanghai decided to send us to England eighteen months before we were really due. At the time we left Chefoo, there was a Japanese commissioner of customs there. He had previously retired to Japan only to be met with a telegram recalling him to China because of the war. I met him one morning in the customs house and he said "You're very lucky to be going home on leave just now — I wish I was doing the same". He did not approve of what his country was doing and he sounded so sad about it all. He once told Christopher that this was the greatest mistake his country had ever made — as it subsequently turned out to be.

We had previously planned to go home via Siberia on the Trans-Siberia railway which would have been so interesting but with the situation as it was in North China we had to change our plans and go south to Hong Kong by coastal ship and pick up a P. & O. liner. On board the coastal ship were many wealthy Chinese families fleeing from the north — some of them had all their wealth in kerosene cans which they kept by their side. They played 'cut in' mah-jong which went on all day and all night.

Chapter 4

HOME LEAVE — RETURN — EVACUATION

We left Hong Kong with a great sense of pleasure at the thought of seeing our families again after five years. The weather had been good and we enjoyed the sea trip but decided to leave the ship at Marseilles and go by train to Paris and so avoid the Bay of Biscay.

Going ashore at Colombo a couple asked me if we were Australian — they thought we might be because of the very dirty old hat that Christopher was wearing. At the time this horrified me and I decided that he could not arrive in England in his precious hat so I threw it out of the carriage window travelling across France. It was some time before Christopher forgave me the loss of his old favourite! After a night in Paris we went on to London where we were met by my family.

Christopher went immediately down to his parents in Wales, and Patricia and I stayed in a hotel in London with my parents. We felt that we should have a headquarters of our own for some of the time, so while he was away, I searched the magazine *'The Lady'* and found just the thing, a cottage called "The Birds Nest" at Nettlebed which the owner Mrs. Finch wished to lease. It was near Henley-on-Thames and a very convenient spot for us, near to London and on the way to Wales.

Before renting 'The Bird's Nest' we all went to Wales to see the Briggs family. We enjoyed the Welsh countryside and Patricia had many new experiences — she rode her first pony and her grandfather gave her her first fishing rod to try her luck in the river Aeron at Aberagron, Cardiganshire. While staying with Uncle Godfrey Briggs at 'Peny-wern', about five miles from Aberystwyth, she saw her first cow being milked which caused a problem — she complained that she always had her milk out of a bottle and did not like the idea of cow's milk. So in future her milk was brought to her in a milk bottle instead of a jug and gradually the problem disappeared.

One day we were taken to tea with a Mrs. Powell who lived in a very large old house called 'Nanteos' not far inland from Aberystwyth.

Mrs. Powell was quite a personality. She was very deaf and had to be spoken to through a large trumpet. She had lost her husband and only son in the 1914-18 war and lived alone in this great big house full of history and antiques. Every bedroom had a four-poster bed with old tapestry curtains, and the 'loo' had the longest walk to it that I have ever taken in a house, you opened the door and at the far end of the narrow passage up a step was a beautifully polished wood seat complete with the old brass-handled pull-up flush, also shining bright. It must have been a very cold spot in the winter! The stables and outside buildings were massive with their cobblestone yards and kennels for a pack of hounds.

The most interesting story of 'Nanteos' was the Holy Cup, or Grail, that was treasured here. This story called 'The Mystery of Glaston' was written by F. B. Bond in 1938. The legend says that Joseph of Arimathea collected the blood of Jesus' side in a wooden cup when he was transfixed with a spear, the cup being the one he had used at the Last Supper. This cup was taken by Joseph to Britain and before his death was confided by him to a nephew at Glastonbury. There it stayed until King Henry VIII dissolved the monasteries in 1529. The monks took it for safety to a monastery in the Welsh mountains called Strata Florida, where for a time it was safe. Eventually the monks had to flee to Ireland and they went via Aberystwyth. Before they got to Aberystwyth they rested at the house of 'Nanteos' with the Powell family and rather than risk the loss of the cup on the sea voyage, they left it in their keeping — where it still remained four hundred years later. For years, the cup was used in healing haemorrhages, and latterly they found that it healed epilepsy. Mrs. Powell told us that at first they allowed it to be taken to the patient, but bits of the edge were bitten off to keep as relics, so a silver rim was put round to protect it but this stopped the power of healing. Then it was placed in a glass fingerbowl and people had to go to Nanteos to drink from it. We were shown a large camphorwood box which was full of letters from people who over the centuries had received healing. In 1938, the last letter in the box was from a boy who was cured of epilepsy.

In 1972 we were told that Nanteos was in the hands of the National Trust but there was some dissension as to what should be done with the cup. Mrs. Powell had not wanted it used for monetary gain, or put in a museum where it could not be used for healing and we were told that it is in safe hands in the keeping of descendants of the Powell family, in England, the whereabouts being a well-kept secret from the outside world.

After our visit to Wales we took up residence at 'The Bird's Nest', Nettlebed, taking Christopher's mother there with us. It was nice to have a home to invite our friends and relatives to such a delightful part of the country. Nettlebed is a small village with a real old-fashioned village green. The plan of the house was quite good but it was not well-built and very draughty — we had to hang a rug over the door to a built-in cupboard in our bedroom to keep out the draught! Later we took Mrs. Briggs back to Wales in the first new car we had ever owned. From Wales we set off on a tour of Scotland and north England, something neither of us had ever been able to do before.

Before leaving Chefoo I had a pair of warm slacks made for the ship. We went to say 'goodbye' to Christopher's father who, on seeing me, said "You are not taking the girl round England in those comic-opera pants?". As we left the house Mrs. Briggs said quietly to me "You will take them off before arriving at Great Auntie Emmie's, won't you dear". Aunt Emmie was over 90, bedridden, and lived alone with her daughter in a very beautiful old black-and-white Tudor house at Scorton, Lancashire. We were later arriving than expected and were shown straight up to see Great Auntie Emmie with no chance for me to change! I stood as near the end of the bed as I could and after a while Great-aunt Emmie said "What a sensible outfit to be travelling in"!! So I felt that I had not completely disgraced the family.

Next day we spent our night near Gretna Green in the very small tent my brother had lent us. The ground was hard to sleep on but we woke to a beautiful misty morning on the moors near a stream where we washed our breakfast utensils and then went on to Glasgow to the Empire Exhibition, driving through the old cobble streets.

This was the second of the great British Empire Exhibitions that drew visitors from all over the world.

When we returned to our lodgings we found that another couple had joined the household and the hostess had a delicious supper waiting for us all and, late as it was, we had a most interesting evening talk. Next morning we had breakfast with bannocks and Scottish bread with the really wonderful Scottish hospitality which we have never forgotten.

From Glasgow our next stop was at Thurso near John O'Groats. In the morning we discovered that the owner of the hotel and his wife had lived in Shanghai and we had many mutual friends. How 'small' the world can be! We then travelled west through lovely highland scenery and saw the shaggy highland cattle.

On our way south we stayed the night at Newcastle — at the time of the Munich crisis — and I remember hearing in the morning a newspaper boy shouting the ominous headlines.

We all gathered again at Nettlebed but my father was anxious to get back to London as quickly as possible to get his uniform out of mothballs. He had been through the Boer War and the Great War and he felt he must be ready for whatever was to come.

We drove back on the Great West Road and saw all the big factories frantically digging dugouts in the gardens in front of their buildings. Then Mr. Neville Chamberlain came back from Munich with 'Peace in our time' and things settled down and the situation seemed more hopeful.

There was a well-known girls' school at Wallingford near Nettlebed run by the Misses Hedges. It was a small boarding school and seemed just the place for Patricia to have the schooling and companionship of her own age that she had missed so much in China. It was hard to leave her and I howled my eyes out when I got home, but that night Miss Hedges wrote me a card which I received the next morning, telling me not to worry as Patricia had settled in well and I was very grateful for her sensitivity. In the September of 1938 Patricia started her schooling and the beginning of a very chequered education for her.

My family came from London to spend Christmas with us. It was a real 'white' Christmas with the huge fir trees weighed down with snow. Patricia was very much in keeping with the scenery in her black velvet coat and bonnet trimmed with white fur and made by my mother.

Christmas was a perfect 'Christmas Card' day. The postman arrived on a bicycle with a sackful of parcels, a cheery man who was given the customary glass of port and no doubt he was warmer and cheerier by the time he had finished his rounds. Nowadays the idea of a delivery on Christmas is sadly missing as it all added to the air of expectation and friendliness, especially for the children.

My Aunt Lina elected to cook the turkey while we were all at church. The kitchen had one of those coal stoves which did the cooking — heated the water and warmed through to the sitting-room on the other side of the wall. It was quite effective but the oven was very small and we came back to find Aunt Lina with the turkey out in the snow trying to put out the fire! There was not enough room and the 'parsons nose' had pressed against the roof of the oven causing the turkey to catch alight.

Sadly the time came when I had to start packing and thinking what we needed to take back to China — things for the house — including some of the Briggs family silver — all of which we were later to lose for ever. We had the rounds of 'goodbyes' to make to family and friends, some we were never to see again including my father and my mother-in-law. So our wonderful leave ended in March 1939.

We left Southampton on the *"Queen Mary"* bound for New York. Our cabin was a luxurious 3 berth, with its own bathroom, writing desk and every comfort. Aunt Lina came down to see us off and as she sat in front of the enormous dressing-table she looked round and said "What a difference to the crowded 'Bird-Cage' that your grandmother travelled in to India". In those days all the women and children were together in one large cabin. I little knew that I was to see plenty of that type of living on sea and land in the not so distant future. On board the *"Queen Mary"* were many European Jews fleeing from the terror that they sensed was coming but thankfully unaware of the terrible things in store for their people. I have often wondered if they were all allowed to land in the U.S. as many had no proper papers.

We spent 24 hours in New York and took Patricia to the Bronx zoo. It was a terribly hot March day and I felt very uncomfortable in a new Scottish tweed suit. I felt equally sorry for the animals in the zoo who were trying so hard to open the water taps to get a drink.

From New York we went by train to Montreal to pick up the Canadian Pacific Railway to Vancouver. It was an interesting and beautiful trip through the snow-covered Rocky Mountains. We stopped at Winnipeg and got out to stretch our legs and the cold was bitter. Patricia was wearing a camel-hair coat and bonnet and long socks with only her knees bare but the cold was so intense that it brought tears to her eyes. After Winnipeg we came to the plains of Alberta and seen at sunrise they were most beautiful. The train was coal-burning and everything was very dirty and when we arrived at Vancouver we were all glad of a bath.

We had four restful days in Vancouver visiting friends and making trips to the parks, but we were too early for the spring flowers.

Three things stand out in my memory of Vancouver, firstly the choice of delicious rolls for breakfast at the comfortable hotel we stayed at, secondly the method of heating the houses by means of vents in the tiles round the rooms with hot air coming up through the floors which was most effective. A similar method to one we had seen in the ruins of a Roman villa we visited in Somerset and surely could be used more widely in presentday homes. Thirdly the frightening experience of walking on a suspension footbridge over a very deep ravine with Patricia bouncing at the far end while we were standing in the middle!

We left Vancouver on the *'Empress of Russia'* for Shanghai and at 6 a.m. one morning we docked at Yokohama. We were interested to see our ship unloading a large cargo of aluminium ingots, no doubt they were to be used to make aeroplanes for the coming war.

On arriving in Shanghai Christopher reported at the customs house and learnt that he was posted to a ship in Hong Kong. Arriving there we went to the old Peninsular Hotel in Kowloon while we were flat-hunting. We were greeted by Patricia's amah Ah Koi, and it was wonderful to see her again all smiles. True to Chinese 'bamboo wireless' she had made sure of finding out our movements and most probably would have turned up in Shanghai if we had been posted there.

We were fortunate to be able to rent the comfortable and roomy house belonging to Harry and Sophie Odell at Homuntin Hill, Kowloon, while they were on leave. When they returned we found a flat at Eu Gardens opposite the Kowloon Hospital. It was bright and very modern with three bedrooms and three bathrooms and plenty of fitted cupboards and wardrobes. For the first time in our married life we bought our own beds, chairs, and dining-suite, the only extra furniture we needed.

While we were at Eu Gardens I got dysentery for the second time but I was put into hospital immediately and was not there long. We will never forget that day — 3rd September 1939 — and as I stepped into my hospital bed news came over the radio that we were at war with Germany — a most dramatic moment and I did not appreciate being in hospital when everyone was so worried. The hospital staff immediately started talking of 'blackout' curtains and one felt one might be bombed at any moment.

We had a Christmas tree that year which looked particularly lovely in the firelight and looking down the passage one evening I caught a glimpse of a little American friend of Patricia's coming into the room to put a present for her by the tree — a picture that 'hangs' in my memory — everything was very peaceful and what lay ahead was still in the unknown. We had a happy time at Eu Gardens and it was to be our last Christmas together for many years.

The customs ships had not been operating since the Sino-Japanese war and Christopher's work had been very restricted. After war broke out with Germany in 1939 it seemed necessary to re-think our plans, and after much debate Christopher and other marine customs officers decided to resign and 'join up'. This of course meant giving up our nice flat and moving to one that we could afford on our much lower naval pay. We took a couple of naval officers as 'boarders' to help financially.

Patricia was attending a small school and I was busy rolling bandages for the Red Cross and passing my first-aid and home-nursing exams. Unfortunately chicken-pox broke out at Patricia's school so I kept her at home counting the days of the incubation period carefully. All went well with her and she returned to school but on that very morning I had ignored a small blister on my neck never having thought that I might develop chicken-pox. By the evening I felt very sick and had a rash all over my tummy. This was disaster for the Red Cross as all the material that I had touched had to be sterilized, much to everyone's annoyance!

In June 1940 we had sudden orders for all service wives and families to be evacuated at thirty-six hours notice — not much time to pack and plan. So it was 'on the move again' for Patricia and me.

As I write this, looking back, I shudder to think what all this entailed and I think 'What a life!', but at the time one just accepted that it had to be done.

On sailing day in July 1940 we were told to be on board the *'Empress of Asia'* at 8 a.m. It was very crowded with all the service wives and families. There were people lying in the corridors and all the cabins were full to overflowing with two or three families in each, according to size. I was fortunate to share a 1st class cabin with another family and we sailed into the tail end of typhoon and I was as sea sick as usual. Later I heard that we had a naval escort as far as Manila but I knew nothing of what was going on at the time. We were a forlorn-looking lot arriving at Manila in the early morning — raining as it can only rain in Manila. What marvellous joy to see my New Zealand friend Iris who had been waiting for us for hours, as she reckoned that Patricia and I would be on board.

Iris was the kind soul who had met us both when we first arrived in Hong Kong. Her husband then was Jim Skinner, also an officer in the Chinese Customs Service. She had since remarried to a Dutchman, Naut Ramondt, and I had quite forgotten they were in Manila where he was manager of the K.L.M. steamship line. They took us to stay in their home and were wonderful to us both for the time we were there.

The afternoon that we landed Iris took us to the American Army Headquarters where all our luggage had been taken. I located mine and was told it would be delivered that day. The day wore on and the rain increased and at eleven p.m. all the dogs barked and we thought it was burglars, which would not have been unusual, but it was a very wet American soldier delivering my luggage as promised. I thanked him and said "I hope that is your last delivery" and he replied "No mam, this is my first". The Americans were really marvellous to us — they did the very best they could at 36-hours notice. Everybody had accommodation, even if it was not all they expected — the luggage was sorted and delivered on schedule and they even had baby food for the babies. They must have been hard put to accommodate 3-4,000 women and children at such short notice and I was sorry to hear so much criticism from my own nationals.

Patricia and I spent a month with the Ramondts. Iris had been a physical instructor and also taught dancing. We used to go round to the Manila Club where she taught Patricia to dive and swim and she was making very good progress.

At the end of the month 'the powers that be' had decided what to do with us all — we were to go to Australia. Two Dutch ships were brought to Manila from Singapore to take us there. This, I feel was where the evacuation went wrong. The scare that prompted the evacuation in the first place was not the threat of the Japanese but of a Chinese Triad Society that the intelligence found were planning to massacre the foreigners in Hong Kong. This threat had passed before we left for Australia and had they allowed those that wanted to go back, or to Britain or Canada or wherever, I feel sure that they would then have been free to decide for themselves what was the best country for their circumstances, with less hard feelings and heartburnings all round.

One of the Dutch ships was the 'Indrapoera', this carried all the naval families. Patricia and I were most fortunate in staying in a Dutch house as I had met all the Dutch personnel arranging the shipping. They insisted there would be no preferential treatment as far as cabins were concerned as they would be arranged alphabetically. However, when Patricia and I arrived on board we found we had the best cabin on the ship on the Captain's deck, very comfortable with its own bathroom.

The officers and crew were very worried about their families in Holland, and whether they ever saw them again I do not know as the 'Indrapoera' was eventually lost during the war. They were all wonderful to us and the fair young stewardesses took such care of all the children who had their own small dining-room and were well looked after. I felt very ashamed of the behaviour of some of my own nationals who were so rude to these girls. In fact the situation became quite unpleasant. I went into the lounge one evening and was met with

Patricia S.S. Taiping one day out of Manila 1941. This photo was taken from me and held by the Japanese but was later returned.

"What have you been up to?" I asked what they meant. Apparently someone whose feelings had got the better of them had been into the captain's cabin and smeared lipstick and powder all over everything and knowing my cabin was next door my friends jokingly accused me of having a part! Poor man, it must have been one of his most difficult trips.

We went direct from Manila to Cairns without stopping. We were blacked-out at night and sailed without lights in case there were any German raiders in the area. Our arrival in Sydney was greeted with a most unexpected but warm welcome. There were cars to meet us, bunches of flowers, and a band playing on the dock. We were taken to the Bondi Pacific Hotel which was more or less empty at that time of the year. There we sorted ourselves out, some went to relatives or friends and many joined forces and found a house or flat to share. It was not an easy time for any of us but it was a great help that we at least all spoke one 'mother tongue', even if only just!

Patricia and I spent about a week at the Bondi Pacific Hotel and then went to Pymble on the invitation of a cousin of my mother's, Iris O'Reilly, whose daughter Tooks was about Patricia's age.

It was Patricia's first experience of a 'loo down-the-garden-path' and I am afraid she did not take to it very kindly and was most distressed. However, we got over that hurdle — we had to! We had an enjoyable week holiday at Avoca Beach north of Sydney where I had my first experience with a 'chip' heater. I was not very successful with it and had great difficulty in getting enough hot water without suffocating myself!

For the uninitiated a 'chip' heater is a cone-shaped metal device which stands on or near the bath. You stuff paper, chips, cardboard and anything burnable in the firebox underneath, light it, turn on the water and try to keep the fire burning and the water-flow adjusted, and at the same time often coping with dense smoke! It took some practice and an acquired skill to get a hot shower or bath.

After our week at Avoca we returned to Pymble but I felt we needed to be nearer Sydney and a school for Patricia, so we went to stay in Vaucluse Road with a lady called Mrs. Sinclair who was very kind to us both. She lived by herself and was within easy walking of the girl's school Kambala.

I met some very nice friends and second-cousins in the seven months we were in Sydney. One family we made friends with in Vaucluse Road were the Oppens. A nephew of his was a friend of ours in the Chinese Maritime Customs. They had two very nice sons — Richard and Conrad — both a little older than Patricia but they used to play together in their lovely garden. It was enjoyable to sit on their terrace on a Sunday morning watching all the yachts sailing in the harbour.

During the school holidays we went to stay with the Oppens at Bowral. Richard was a keen rider and took part in the riding competitions. While we were at Bowral Patricia fell and broke her arm, but it turned out to be only a green-stick fracture and it healed quickly.

After a while I started battling to return to my home in Hong Kong. It seemed grossly unfair to me that women were being allowed into the Colony who had never lived there before, yet I was not allowed to return to my home. It is a long, sad, and complicated story — Christopher battled from one end and I battled from the other — not always above-board I am afraid. In the end I was allowed to leave Sydney. As I went to get my ticket the assistant said "Well you deserve it Mrs. Briggs, you have battled hard". Little did he know what the future held, nor did I!

The tragic part came when we got to Manila and I received a cable from Christopher saying I must leave Patricia in Manila or I would not be allowed to land. A cousin of Christopher's, Stephen Crawfurd, was manager of the Shell Company in Manila. He and his American wife Maude offered to take Patricia until things settled down and we could make new plans. I need not go into what that decision meant to me and the heartbreak for us both — it is something that I still recoil from and wish it had never happened. It was a deep wrench that has healed over the years but the scars will always remain. The suddeness of it was too severe. I will never forget that night as I sailed away. There was a kindly Armenian couple on board, Theo and Gympy Bagram, and they did their best to help me. I was to see quite a lot of them later during the fall of Hong Kong.

Chapter 5

SAD DAYS IN HONG KONG

On arrival in Hong Kong, I was miraculously allowed ashore though I found out later that I should not have been and from then on I was harassed to leave again. I was told I could only stay if I had a job but was rejected for every job I tried to get as I was a returned evacuee. I began to feel quite ill with worry until a kindly young police officer confided quietly to me one day in police headquarters, that they could not deport me. I brushed up my shorthand and one day saw an advertisement for a secretary to the firm of Dodwell & Co. Ltd., I answered it in fear and trembling and gave my experience, which included the fact that I had been trained at Madame Hoster's in London. It so happened, that the advertiser's personal secretary had also been trained at Hoster's and felt that was a good enough recommendation. I went for an interview, was taken on, and told to report the following Tuesday. It happened to have been a long holiday weekend and the boss of the department, Keith Valentine, a captain in the Hong Kong Volunteer Defence Force, had gone to Fanling to play golf. On Tuesday I turned up as arranged and during the morning Captain Valentine asked to see me. He was a very nice, gently-spoken man and he explained that I should not have been employed as he was head of the evacuation committee! This put him in a very awkward position. However, as I had been taken on in his absence and had started work, he did not want to put me to any more hardship and worry. This was most generous of him and I was very grateful. I worked for Dodwells until the Japanese invasion. Their offices were in the Hong Kong and Shanghai Bank building. It was here that I made friends with a Portugese girl named Elsie Soares. She had red hair and was charming and vivacious, and was to help me greatly later on.

For some months things seemed to go on as usual in Hong Kong. There must have been some underlying uncertainty as I felt I should take the precaution of writing about money matters and family addresses to Stephen Crawfurd, just in case he needed them for Patricia.

He replied, thanking me, and said he would make a note but he was sure the situation was O.K.

The human being has a wonderful defence mechanism to shut out facts he does not want to know — and I think this happened to many of us at that time and I am sure it still does.

On Sunday 7th December, 1941, Christopher and I went for a walk in the hills behind Kowloon — the hills the Japanese were so soon to cross. The volunteers were out training which they had been doing for some time. After our walk, we went home to dinner and discussed the possibility that I should pick Patricia up from Manila and we would go home to England. My father had died in November and I was anxious to go to my mother. Christopher said he would then try to get a transfer and it was left like that, and he returned to duty on H.M.S. *'Scout'* of which he was the first lieutenant. We arranged to meet for lunch at the Hong Kong club next day. Next day (as planned) was one of those days that never happened — it was the fateful Monday, December 8th, 1941.

Ah Koi called me as usual and I had just had my bath when the phone rang at 7 a.m.; it was Christopher ringing from the dockyard to say "We are at war — bring over some clothes when you come", as he put the phone down I heard a plane fly towards Kai Tak aerodrome at the end of our road, and my thought was "At last they have sent some planes from Singapore", then I heard a loud "wump" — it was the Japanese planes bombing Kai Tak and the Pan American Clipper which was anchored in the bay. I went over to the harbour as arranged but Christopher and I could only meet at the dockyard gate for a few minutes. It turned out to be our last meeting for over 3½ years.

In Hong Kong everything was pandemonium and I wandered round not quite knowing where to go or what to do. The bombing was fairly continuous, and one had to rush constantly for shelter. The Food Control Administration asked me to go back to my flat in Kowloon and wait there to be ready to 'man' a food depot that was to be opened quite close to our flat. I called there on my way back to my flat and there was a Chinese gentleman also waiting — but no sign of any food rations — so I went home to await orders.

I went to the food depot again next day but there were no further developments, transport and everything had broken down — many Chinese who had taken on transport in an emergency had disappeared. I then walked down Nathan Road for a couple of miles to see if I could pick up our car which was having some repairs done to it. There were no Europeans to be seen and the Chinese were all milling round in a very confused state as the bombing was so continuous. The car was not ready so I called in to the Peninsular Hotel to see if there was anyone I knew there who could give me news but without any luck. Standing outside wondering what to do I saw a man in a rickshaw stop and he got out and came over to me — he was from the dockyard and on his way to our flat with a letter from Christopher. It was to say "By the time you get this we will have sailed and it may be quite a time before we meet again". My whole being felt numb and I felt very lost.

They had sailed after dark on the Monday night en route to Singapore in company with another of the three Hong Kong destroyers, H.M.S. *'Thanet'*.

I went back to the flat again to do some telephoning and to try and find out what was happening but could not get through to the Food Administration; however, I managed to get through to the naval dockyard to see if they could take some of our valuables and personal effects to store. They said they would call on Thursday morning. I spent all Wednesday packing to have everything ready for collection. I tried to get some sleep that night, but the bombing and noise was terrible and at times I felt the Japanese were just outside the flat. I decided that I could not spend another night alone in the flat and must go over to friends in Hong Kong. I discovered later that I and my two Amahs were the only people in a large block of flats, with the exception of one Chinese couple whom I saw leaving the next morning. I packed an overnight bag — took my money which I had hidden on the top of the boiler — and prepared to leave. Outside, I saw a couple of women in a car who had come to their flat to collect some clothes and I asked them if they would give me a lift to the ferry. While they were collecting their things I told Ah Koi what I was doing and that I would be back first thing next morning and to give the things that I had packed to the dockyard men when they called — (of course they were never able to do this). I told her that she and the young girl must not stay in the flat that night but should go to some Chinese friends.

We had recently been given a very beautiful black Alsatian bitch and I decided that I could neither take her with me or leave her behind. Fortunately, there were some Indian soldiers billeted quite close, so I took her to them and asked them to shoot her. This was too terrible, but something I am always thankful that I had done.

When we got to the ferry, the crowd was terrific. We were bombed all the way as we crossed — they were trying to hit the wireless station at Stonecutters Island quite close to our route. When I got across I found that I had been on the last ferry. On hearing this I was aghast. I tried frantically for some time to get through to Ah Koi by phone to tell her to come over any possible way she could by sampan or motor boat but to my everlasting regret I was never able to get through to her — the line was dead. Since my repatriation, I have tried through various means to locate her but the space of time has made it impossible — I could only go to her village at Shekloong near Canton in hope of hearing some news of her.

I called at the Food Administration Office again to see if I could help in any way — I shall never forget the expression on the face of the man at the desk as I entered — he literally looked as if he had seen a ghost! They had been trying to contact me by phone for two days to tell me to come over to Hong Kong at once. I think they never expected to see me again. There was nothing for me to do at the Food Control Office — things were too chaotic everywhere. I then went to Dodwell's office in the Hong Kong and Shanghai Bank building and from my desk I could see our troops retreating from Kowloon across the harbour. The office was very empty, Elsie Soares the red-headed Portugese girl was there, and she asked me to spend the night with her family on the Peak Road and this I gratefully accepted. During the morning we sheltered in the bank's boiler room when there was a particularly bad air raid. It was marvellously quiet down there but rather warm. I went home with Elsie, and her family were very kind to me. They lived in a lovely old rambling Chinese-style house overlooking the harbour.

I stayed the next night, Friday, 12th December 1941, in the flat belonging to Lieutenant Commander and Mrs. Dawes at 8 Garden Terrace. They were not in the flat and it was very frightening all alone, because by this time the Japanese were shelling as well as bombing and the flat was in a direct line with the Canossa Hospital, which they were trying to hit. Most of our hospitals had the Red Cross sign on the roof but unfortunately were guarded by soldiers and guns which made them a sure target. I presume that this was to prevent the hospitals being used as a refuge by the local public.

Eventually, I learned that when I heard the scream of the shell, it had passed and not hit me! From the verandah of this flat I had a fine view of the harbour and watched the scuttling of H.M.S. 'Tamar'. She was an old warship that had for many years been permanently tied up in the dockyard basin and had been used as depot and accommodation ship. She used to fly the flag of Commodore Hong Kong. Later, I was talking to one of the dockyard policemen who had done the job and he told me that it was fantastic to see the number of rats leaving the sinking ship.

Mrs. Dawes rang me on Saturday morning to go at once to Aberdeen. What a tremendous relief it was to have something to do. Aberdeen is a fishing village round the opposite side of the island to the city and the navy had commandeered the large Industrial School there. I wondered how I was going to get there but a Russian H.K.V.D.C. arrived at the flat next door in his car and he was able to drive me to Aberdeen at once. There had been a lull in the bombing and shelling while a group of Japanese came over the harbour with a white flag to talk with our governor, but he refused to surrender and so the war went on, the bombing and shelling continued.

On arrival at Aberdeen I was detailed to drive personnel to and from Hong Kong dockyard or any other job that needed transport.

The ground floor of the school had been turned into a sick-bay for wounded who were brought in from the surrounding area. One side of a wide corridor running the full length of the building was the sick bay — the other side was a big canteen and kitchen. On the first floor, naval personnel had accommodation and offices. There was another woman driver beside myself, Mrs. Freddie Dalziel. We were billeted in an empty house on Shouson Hill, quite close. Also billeted there were eight men from the wireless station on Stonecutters Island, nine amahs, and twenty-four Indian Army Sikhs. We painted all the windows black against air raids, and the lovely lounge was stacked ceiling high with sacks of rice. It was sad to see this nice house being treated so badly. Freddie and I dragged our mattresses down to the safety of the lounge in the middle of the night as the bombing was so bad. There was just room for the mattress in the centre — but after a while we became very conscious of the weevils from the rice dropping on us!

We reported at the school each morning and one of my first jobs was to take a naval warrant officer to the Hong Kong dockyard. By this time I had been given dockyard dungarees from the stores ('slops') and anything else that I could wear, such as extremely hard and uncomfortable pyjamas, but I was grateful for anything, as I only had my overnight bag and the clothes I stood up in. When I got to the naval dockyard, one of the marines gave me his tin hat — he was horrified to see me with nothing on my head in all that bombing.

On the 17th December I had to pick up Wing Commander Bennett from the Peak and bring him back to Aberdeen. He had a magnificent moustache and was always referred to as 'The Flying Moustache'. It was very eerie up the Peak with not a soul anywhere and I was grateful for my armed guard. It was not considered safe now for women to be driving alone and an armed sailor was detailed to go with us whenever we were called out. The reason for these trips to the Peak was that an underground command post was situated there. They were very unpleasant trips, as the road was exposed to gunfire from across the harbour and one felt very vulnerable.

That afternoon we saw a huge black pall of smoke in the sky over the Peak. I took Commander Millet to see where it was coming from, and we discovered the oil depot at North Point had been hit.

In the evening I was asked to take Wing Commander Bennett back to the Peak. There was no armed guard available and I was not looking forward to the long drive back alone. However, when I got there, a Jesuit priest was very anxious to contact some Chinese boys at Aberdeen and I was certainly most grateful for his company back. I hope he found his Chinese charges.

After breakfast on 18th December I was standing on a small balcony leading from the room on the first floor, that we all used for meals. It seemed quiet and peaceful but as I stood there I heard a different sound towards Wongneichong Gap — the sound of machine-gun fire. This puzzled me, but when Freddie and I reported at the school we found out the reason — the Japanese had landed on the island during the night. We were both taken off the roads and from then on we worked in the sick-bay which became a very busy place with wounded coming in almost continuously. We had strict orders to remove all arms from the men in case the Japanese suddenly appeared in the corridor. The men found this hard to accept and it was quite usual to open a drawer by the bed and find a revolver "To have ready just in case"! The wounded did not stay long at Aberdeen and were transferred to one of the Hong Kong hospitals.

One afternoon two friends of ours were brought in, Lieutenant John Douglas R.N.R. and Lieutenant Commander John Boldero D.S.C. R.N. They had just scuttled their ships and were both in a very distressed state. John Douglas had been temporarily blinded by an explosion from the ship's refrigerator. He was lying on the bed in a stiff shirt and mess dress and I asked him why he was dressed like that, he said "I had to put my best clothes on to do honour to my ship"!

John Boldero was a different case. He had lost an arm in an accident before the war. The strain was catching up with him and the stump of his left arm was giving him great pain. He asked me to get him a drug to relieve the pain. I asked the orderly for something without any luck, so I took him a glass of hot milk and said "Now drink this and you will go to sleep". I talked to him for a while about his family and in a very short time he was fast asleep, satisfied and at peace unaware that there was no drug in the milk. I never saw him again but I heard that he had escaped.

After the Japanese had landed, Freddie Dalziel and I had to sleep at the school as the Shousson Hill house had been evacuated. A kind paymaster, Commander Sisson, went into the bedroom at Shousson Hill and hurriedly snatched anything of ours that was handy. He picked up my overnight bag which contained jewellery and a silver travelling clock — and I still have these articles now, thanks to him.

That evening at 11 p.m. I was woken to go to the sick bay as a number of badly wounded had been brought in, among them men from H.M.S. 'Thracian' whom I had seen going off into the hills in trucks that morning. H.M.S. 'Thracian' was the remaining local defence flotilla destroyer, which had been left behind when the others sailed on the first day of the attack. 'Thracian' had been fitted out for mine-laying and her job was to mine the approaches to Hong Kong in the event of hostilities with Japan but she had been badly damaged and her crew put ashore. The Japanese must have repaired her because months later I saw her sailing past Stanley, flying a Japanese flag. Poor 'Thracian'!

It is strange how one reacts in times of emergency. As I entered the sick-bay that night I saw a man with terrible face wounds and my reaction was 'Oh, no, not that' I found myself walking right through the room in a kind of daze, out through another door and in again at the first door, and as I passed the shattered face again, the naval dentist asked me to help him with the patient. As soon as I started helping my feeling of horror left me and I was able to clean his mouth and make him comfortable. He had been shot in the mouth, and teeth and moustache were very mixed.

One morning, a Japanese woman arrived in the building saying she was the wife of one of the Hong Kong naval reserve officers. She had walked from the Peak down the rugged track on the west side of the island. Nobody seemed to know much about her and we were told to keep careful watch and not leave her alone. A lot of signalling had been seen at times from the Peak. What eventually happened to her I do not know, but I met her husband later in Stanley camp on his own. We certainly appreciated his being there as he was an excellent pianist and kept us all singing 'old-timers' in the evening until we were stopped by the Japanese. We would meet after our meagre meal, crowd into a room where there was a piano and packed like sardines we would sing all the old-timers late into the night. Our spirit was something the Japanese could not understand.

On the 22nd December 1941 at 4.30 a.m. the captain sent word that Freddie Dalziel and I, with all the patients, were to leave at first light in the R.A.F. ambulance for the Queen Mary Hospital in hope of getting through without being ambushed. Fortunately, we got through but there were signs that there had been fighting on that road. The rest of that night until daylight, I sat talking to a group of fifteen Canadians, part of the battalion of the Winnipeg Grenadiers who had landed two weeks before the attack to swell our small army forces. They had received a great welcome as they marched up Nathan Road, Kowloon, and it had made us feel more secure. The men I was talking to had found their way down tracks from the Peak to the Industrial School. They were 'lost' in more ways than one — they never had time to become familiar with the terrain of the island and had lost many of their men. It was a sad talk and a very tragic episode in the lives of those few Canadians who were left.

About this time fighting all over the island was spreading and fierce fighting took place at the lovely resort of Repulse Bay on the far side of the island from the city of Victoria. Today there are a number of houses and blocks of flats on the hillside but at the time war broke out in 1941 the only buildings on the bay were the well-known and well-loved Repulse Bay Hotel, with its tropical and peaceful atmosphere, and 'Eucliff' built on the edge of a cliff in the style of a small medieval castle by Mr. Eu, a Chinese millionaire who had a great admiration for things English or European, although he had never been to Europe. Along the pleasant beach were the 'matsheds' owned by the different firms or associations, or by private individuals, where one could take one's picnic lunch or dinner — enjoy a swim and come back to sit in comfort under the matting roof. A 'matshed' consisted of a wooden floor with side and roof of palms. They varied in size according to one's pocket. Chairs and tables could be locked up and left in the care of a watchman.

At the time of the invasion we had no knowledge of what was happening at Repulse Bay on the 22nd December (the time we left Aberdeen) but later I was to hear the full tragedy of that lovely spot.

In the terrible confusion and continual bombing families were arriving in the colony from northern ports trying to get ashore from their ships not knowing where to go or what to do. Some managed to get to Repulse Bay where they hoped it might be quieter and safer. For the next few days this move seemed justified and the hotel remained an oasis of peace.

By 17th December the Japanese were penetrating into the hills and many of our troops found they were fighting without food and water. In due course they fell back on the hotel for sustenance, thereby making a fortress out of it. By 19th December there were some 300 British troops and volunteers in the hotel. The Japanese had taken possession of the garage some 150 yards away and were completely encircling the hotel from the hills. The siege now started in earnest. From the mountain behind the hotel a large tunnel was discovered running under the hotel and out to the beach. For 5 days and nights the women and children were huddled in this dark and insanitary tunnel while the men attempted to bring them food, being continually sniped at while crossing the open space between the hotel and the tunnel entrance.

At midnight on 22nd December orders were received to surrender the hotel, so under the cover of darkness the troops left in two parties, making for Stanley fort at the end of the peninsula. The first party got through but the second was ambushed on the tortuous road and badly cut to pieces. With these two parties went many of the civilians who had no family at the hotel. The remaining civilians proceeded to destroy all stocks of liquor on the premises. At day break continual firing broke out all round and they could hear the Japanese shouting to each other, evidently afraid to approach for fear of an ambush. One of the party who spoke Japanese called out to them and presently several advanced with fixed bayonets and rifles at the ready. They seemed genuinely surprised that no soldiers were present and the men were promptly rounded up and cross-examined. The following morning they were paraded and for three hours many particulars were laboriously written down. They were then given five minutes to pack a suitcase each and the party of some 150, without having eaten, were marched towards the Wan Chai Gap and thence to Taikoo docks — a journey of about 10 miles. At Taikoo docks they were handed over to the Japanese gendarmerie. The party by this time was completely exhausted and were left for several hours on the open pavement guarded by sentries. Water and food were refused until 6 p.m. On Christmas morning they breakfasted on a few scraps left over from the night before and at mid-day were bundled into lorries and taken down to the docks where they waited some two hours. There was intermittent shelling from British guns and for once they hoped that their aim would be inaccurate. Eventually they were taken over to the Kowloon Hotel, now devoid of all furniture. Suddenly they noticed that all firing had ceased but it was some hours before news filtered through that the colony had surrendered.

The party was kept there for a month on a diet consisting of a bowl of rice and a glass of water twice a day — doors and windows were sealed and pasted over and any attempt to open them was punishable by court-martial and being shot. After a month of this existence the party was taken by sea under armed escort to Stanley Peninsula to join 2,000 prisoners from other parts of the island. A small family of three — a couple and a three year old child — who had found short solace at Repulse Bay now shared with forty-five others a bungalow built to accommodate five persons at the most.

To return to my own movements on 22/23rd December. The night of the 22nd merged into the early hours of the 23rd and seemed the longest and loneliest day in my life.

I quote from a few faded notes I made at that time:-

"Casualties all day — Chinese from village and our own. Terrible night. Got up at 2 a.m. Canadian R.A.M.C. brought in 15 men from Mt. Cameron — wanted to get transport to take them to Bowen Road — refused as condition of road unknown. 4.30 a.m. Commander Montague sent orders to evacuate all patients at daybreak — also us two women (Freddie Dalziel had permission not to go for personal reasons). We left in R.A.F. ambulance wondering how far we would get or if we would see any Japanese but saw only a few bodies. Left patients at Queen Mary Hospital — returned in ambulance that was going to the dairy farm (below hospital). They said I must not stay as they all slept at the hospital — went back there but they would not take me in and told me to apply in town at transport office — ironical!!! Met Commander Minhinick outside hospital and went back with him to Aberdeen — a lot of bombing — something nearly hit us as we neared Aberdeen. Had 'tiffin' (lunch) Aberdeen — situation said to be well in hand — line right across island — shelling worse than ever — keeping no patients there. Returned with Commander Minhinick to Queen Mary Hospital — uncertainty everywhere — bomb fell in front of hospital while there — Mrs. Selwyn Clarke sent me to Sister Gordon at University — got lift in car to lower steps — a Portugese soldier carried my bag up miles of steps. Relief to get into quieter atmosphere – shelling all night.

24th December — started nursing Chinese in hall at University. I was given a room to myself at the University which was a relief. I fell into bed that first night absolutely exhausted and tried to relax. I turned round towards the wall and with no warning whatsoever was violently sick — I felt dreadful. There was a knock at my door and a little Russian lady — a complete stranger — came in great distress — she had heard me and wanted to help me. I was very grateful to her as she gave me the care and attention that I needed so desperately just then. My sickness was nothing more than the result of shock.''

The reason the suggestion for me to go to the transport office was 'ironical' was because Dr. Selwyn Clarke (later Sir Selwyn Clarke) told me, when I offered my services before war started, that he did not need me for transport as he had plenty of Chinese drivers. He and I were not on the best of terms anyway. But at this later date he was hard-put for drivers as none of the Chinese he had expected turned up when needed.

I worked for 24 hours with chronically sick Chinese lying on camp stretchers or on the floor in a large hall. They had been turned out of Chinese hospitals to make room for their wounded. There was no hot water and it was not very pleasant. Later our own wounded were brought to one of the University buildings and I transferred to nursing them until they were eventually moved to the military or naval hospitals and subsequently to prison camp. There were no lights by which to attend to them — only saucers of peanut oil with a wick of string placed on chairs or tables, and very messy when they were upset.

One afternoon a man from the naval dockyard was brought in with a very sore throat and possible pneumonia feeling utterly miserable. He said to me "If only I could get a dirty sock to put round my neck". A rather odd request but I remembered one of my aunts swearing by this treatment as a wonderful cure, so I hunted round for a dirty sock and put it round his neck and he was happy! I never knew if this cured his sore throat but he was psychologically at peace which was important.

Most of our men had no personal belongings, only very hard unbleached cotton pyjamas issued by the hospital, and for men peppered by bursting hand-grenades they caused great discomfort.

On Christmas Day 1941 I went round to all the naval personnel and made a list of their names to see if I could get some of their kit from the naval dockyard. I then rang Lieutenant Commander Dawes in the afternoon with my request, and his answer came "My dear, we have just surrendered" — I could not believe it — I just felt numb and horrified. Next morning Japanese officers came into the ward, the air was very tense but fortunately the control by our men was wonderful and nothing terrible happened.

When our men were removed from the University I was interned at the main building with about forty others in May Hall, which became a place of refuge for us for about a month. I was fortunate because so many Europeans from other districts were taken to empty Chinese hotels or brothels and they had a very unpleasant time.

The Bagrams (Theo and Gympy) whom I had met on the ship coming from Australia, were also at the University. As soon as we realized that eventually we would be sent to the internment camp at Stanley, Gympy and I started to organize ourselves. There was a storeroom and we were given the key and permission to distribute the sheets, grey army blankets, towels, soap, tins of coconut oil, and many things that would be invaluable to us in camp. These we divided as best as we could among those who were going from the University and had so little to take with them. There were also a few camp-stretchers, but not enough to go round, so we asked the Chinese students still living at the University and using camp-stretchers if they would be willing to exchange with those of us who had iron beds. They very kindly agreed to this which meant that we could give each person a camp-stretcher to take into Stanley. Some of the professors' wives gave us clothes. I was still wearing my dockyard dungarees and was delighted to be given a pair of grey flannel slacks, a couple of blouses, and a small sized coat-and-skirt. I am 5ft. 8½" and the lady who owned them was about 5ft. 2". Somehow I was able to alter the clothes to fit and arrived in Liverpool nearly four years later squeezed into the coat-and-skirt! (I still had my pair of hand-made Chefoo shoes, having mostly gone barefoot in camp with the result that the soles of my feet were so tough that if I trod on a chip of gravel it was well embedded before I felt it and consequently very difficult to dig out.)

The fatal day dawned on Saturday, 31st January 1942, when we had to move to Stanley and live behind a barbed-wire fence. Our month at the University in comparative isolation was at an end. We were to travel by truck, and much to our surprise the Japanese gave us permission to take our precious stretchers. Most of us had painted our names on the canvas in large letters. We were all ready with as much luggage as we could carry and our beds rolled up and on the second truck. We were sitting waiting to start when the Japanese suddenly decided that we could not take our stretchers — this seemed the last straw! However, somebody must have had a great power of persuasion because, after a lot of arguing and discussion, they promised to send them to us next day. We had to be content with that promise but never thought we would see our beds again and left feeling very depressed. We arrived at Stanley early afternoon and eventually were given our billets.

A small group of men came to help us carry our belongings and take us to our various billets. I looked round for a familiar face but could not see one and felt very lonely and lost, rather like the first day at school in a playground where you knew nobody but now one knew there was no loving home and comforts to return to, just complete loneliness. Then I spotted a face I recognized from a brief meeting some months previously in the Police Station at the time when, as a returned evacuee, I was being harassed by the police to leave the Colony. I was so grateful to see a friendly face in that strange and alien surrounding and a friendship sprang up that meant much to me and was to help me greatly to come to terms with the unreal life of internment. We were "ships that passed in the night" and at once we recognised something other than just darkness at sea. Though I do not identify this person in the remainder of this story I have always been full of gratitude for that (chance?) meeting and I include this small incident in the hope that it will be read by the person concerned.

At that time we were all sure our internment would be a matter of weeks not years.

My first night was spent uncomfortably on a cement floor with just a thin blanket under me. Next morning to our joy and amazement our camp stretchers arrived! Their promise had been kept.

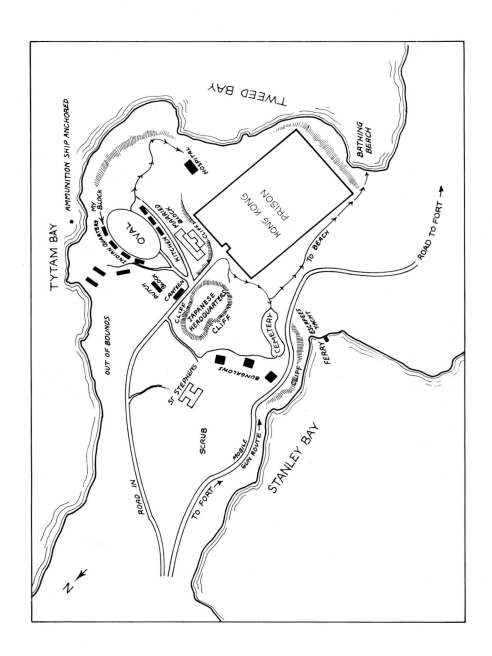

Chapter 6

INTERNMENT — SURVIVAL — RELEASE

For the first two months at Stanley I was living in the Indian warder's quarters (flats) with six complete strangers. There were four men in one room and two women in the smaller room, myself making three. I sensed that for some reason they all resented me and I was not at all happy there, except that I got a little extra to eat as one of the men worked in the kitchen and brought back fish heads in his gumboots! I found the bowls of fish heads most revolting with their eyes goggling.

The two women used to lie and whisper to each other late into the night and one of them sometimes returned very late. This and their resentment at my presence was explained later when one evening a man came to the door of the flat at 5 p.m. and left a message with me for one of the men who at that time was out. The same evening this man and one of my room-mates escaped with three others. They sailed in a yacht that had been beached in a bay in view of the camp. Another couple on the same night decided to escape overland to China.

Mrs. Gwen Priestwood, who escaped overland, was able to give Christopher news of me when she arrived in Bombay. Had I known of her plans before she left I would have sent a message but neither of us knew each other previously so naturally I would not have been told of the escape plans and she did not know that my husband was in Bombay.

The Japanese did not discover the escapes until next morning so the escapees had a good start. This caused great consternation when the Japanese found out. We all had to stay in our rooms and be questioned and searched. There were no repercussions except a curfew and roll-call which lasted the rest of our internment.

My remaining room-mate at that time was Elma Kelly, an Australian journalist. She had brought a chicken into camp in the hope of a few extra eggs to supplement her diet. It was a rather miserable specimen and I would wake in the morning to see a wary eye looking at me from the same level as my bed! It's owner used to tie a string round one leg and take it onto the football oval for exercise and green feed. Sadly it turned out to be a cock and was put into somebody's stew! She had not the heart to eat it herself.

About this time I was given permission to move my accommodation and was very grateful for this. I was still living in the Indian warder's quarters, and my new flat-mates were Nell Hale, Mrs. Scotcher and for a short time her daughter Peggy all in my room. I was to stay here until the end of the war.

In the smaller room was Frankie Innes, whose husband, Major Leslie Innes R.E., was in Shamshuipo P.O.W. camp on the mainland. He had been instrumental in the building of the Shingmun dam. He was later taken to Japan in the 'Lisbon Maru' which was sunk en route and he lost his life with so many others. Poor Frankie did not hear of this till we arrived at Manila after our release.

Also in the smaller room was Pat Fox. Pat was only 24 at the time of our internment. She had not been married very long to Jack Fox, an officer in the Middlesex Regiment, when tragically he was killed during the fighting in Hong Kong. She needed, and had, great courage to carry her through that sad time.

The flats consisted of two cement floored rooms which opened onto a small verandah in front and a narrow passage at the back, one end of which was a place to cook with a large cement slab on which to stand a 'chatti'. A 'chatti' is an earthenware stove in which the Chinese burn charcoal, but if one is compelled to use grass the result is absolutely suffocating.

The other end of the passage was a Chinese W.C. which took a little getting used to. For the uninitiated a Chinese (or oriental) W.C. consists of a small porcelain bowl sunk level to the cement floor with two footrests each side with roughened surface. Squatting over this and rising again was not easy until one got used to it. I managed by gripping onto the window catch which I hoped would stand up to the strain!

Squatting is really the natural position to be in and if we always used this method there would be less complaints of constipation and haemorrhoids. There was a cistern to flush, also a small basin with water tap. I used to stand over the W.C. and shower with cold water, using a rubber hosepipe fixed to the tap.

I had only two hot washes in 3½ years. A kind friend managed to get a bucket of boiling water from the communal kitchen and carry it all the way to our block. First I washed myself with a loofa (borrowed from one of the Matilda Hospital sisters in the flat below) to get a good scrub — then I washed my clothes — and last gave my sheet a 'freshener — all in the same bucket of water! It was marvellous and I felt really clean. Lack of soap was a nightmare and when I got down to a piece the size of a 20 cent piece and had no idea where the next was coming from, I felt quite ill. We never knew when there would be a canteen and many of us had no money unless we had some gold to sell. I sold my signet engagement ring and a gold bracelet my grandmother had given me.

The Indian families were living in their quarters up until the time we moved in, when they moved out. We had strict instructions not to have any dealings with the Indians still there; some of them were friendly but some of them were not and could report one to the Japanese. It was a difficult and tense time for all of us. However, the word got round that the Indians were willing to deal with us, so one evening I decided to risk it and went up after dark to a room on the first floor where a number of Indians were smoking their waterpipes. Through a haze I conducted my purchase of a small basket table. It was in good condition and fitted nicely at the head of my bed. I now had two pieces of furniture — a camp bed and a table — and later I was given a piece of wood taken from a desk at St. Stephen's College. I fixed this to the wall as a shelf above my bed. With these three items I felt quite well furnished.

One day soon after we were interned we were all ordered to a large square outside the gaol gates and told to take nothing with us. We stood for two hours in intermittent rain surrounded by armed Japanese, not knowing our fate or what was happening to our few possessions left behind. The women were searched by Chinese women-warders and the men by Japanese soldiers. After another long wait we were told to return to our rooms. What joy to find that nothing had been taken except my precious tin hat given me by a dockyard policeman during the fighting. They were searching for radios and cameras. How glad I was that I had made a cotton belt with pockets lined with cotton wool for my few pieces of jewellery and my wedding ring, that I had reluctantly taken off for the first time since our marriage. I wore the belt round my waist whenever there was a search. In the early days wedding rings were being snatched from the women by the Japanese, and for 3½ years I wore a replacement ring made on a home made lathe by a Mr. Raven, aged 73 and the oldest internee. He made many of these rings while in camp by punching out the centre of a Hong Kong 10 cent piece. I still have this ring in my possession.

Two months after I entered Stanley I discovered a lump on my breast which was most distressing. I went at once to see Dr. James Smalley and he advised the removal of the lump.

The Queen Mary Hospital staff had been brought to Stanley by launch from Pokfulam, together with a quantity of equipment, not nearly enough but it was wonderful to have any. We also had staff and doctors from the Kowloon Hospital across the harbour.

We waited two weeks for dry dressings to come into camp owing to the difficulty of dealing with the Japanese. When the dressings arrived Dr. James Smalley operated without delay, but while operating he decided he should perform a mastectomy. This was a great shock to me when he told me next day what he had done. By the time I arrived in England 3½ years later I had, to a great extent, become reconciled to what had happened to me. Then I had to go through the trauma a second time in telling my husband and family what had happened to a most sensitive and important part of a woman's body and the terrible feeling of being incomplete.

I was fortunate to be operated on by the talented surgeon Dr. Smalley whom I knew well. He was a speedy and efficient surgeon and I owe him a deep debt of gratitude as he was not in the best of health in camp.

I haemorrhaged very badly and of course there was no drug to give me. One of the sisters washing my sheets said to herself "Poor thing that patient is a gonner". She did not know me at the time but I met her later.

The operation was successful but five weeks after I had left hospital and ten weeks after the operation the 'negative' report was received and I learnt that the operation need never have been performed!

The building used as a hospital was long and narrow and had been used for Indian bachelor staff. There were two long rooms, downstairs for male patients and upstairs for women. It was full of patients when I went in with just standing room between each bed. There was nothing in the way of blood transfusions or other emergency measures if they were needed. The nurses worked very hard on their low diet. They had all the washing of the hospital linen besides the nursing, and no washing machines, just buckets.

After the operation I was told to get up and walk to the W.C. There was nobody free to help me and I just burst into tears, but I found on arrival that a makeshift wooden seat had been made to stand over the Chinese W.C. It was not at all pleasant and rather rickety, but it was a great help to anyone who found it painful to move and I was thankful for it.

The tremendous shock of all that had happened in the preceeding weeks had caused the cessation of my monthly cycle, as it had done many other young women. This meant that they became very fat and 'puffy' on a rice diet which was very distressing. Immediately after my operation things for me became normal again. The second shock seemed to undo the first.

Nell Hale was a sick person from the early days in camp right through to the end. She had beri-beri badly and suffered a great deal with swollen and painful legs and was unable to bear covering over her feet at night. When she could not sleep she used to light a cigarette (if she was fortunate to have one) until she discovered that the smell always woke me and then she smoked her cigarette on the verandah; she was a very caring person. A Chinese she knew in Hong Kong managed to send in a trunk of hers with many useful belongings from sewing material to eiderdowns, and she shared so much of this with those in need. For me it was the eiderdown which was beyond price.

The first Allied air raid over Hong Kong was on the 15th October 1942. At 1.30 a.m. we were rocked by an explosion — things fell off the shelves — and in the dark people wandered round not knowing what had happened. Next morning a ship which had been anchored in Taitam Bay quite close to us, had left and subsequently we heard it was an ammunition ship, so if it had been hit, I would not be here today and I am very thankful of the 'miss'. Later on at night we could faintly hear the drone of planes at great heights as they passed deep into China, and we used to wonder where they came from and where they were going. One guessed they were American planes and we all listened in silence, knowing there were friends trying to help and it gave us a wonderful feeling. Whenever I hear the drone of a plane high overhead, I remember those nights of listening and praying that they would get safely through their task.

When daylight raids started, sirens used to scream and everyone had to run for shelter wherever they were or they would be shouted at and have shots fired at them. One day, I had been to collect the midday meal for myself and my five flatmates. I had two tins per person, ten tins in all, which took a bit of managing — rice in one, soup and strings of lettuce slop in the other. Suddenly the air raid siren went as I was leaving the kitchen so I decided to make a dash for my block which was at the far end of the football oval. I had almost made it when I heard a thud in the ground near me. That was nearly the end of all my five lunches. I had been shot at by a sentry. I was lucky to be opposite a door in another block and got inside as fast as I could, a bit shaky, but grateful that I had been missed.

One evening I was walking by myself looking for scraps of wood to burn. I was on the side of the square opposite the gaol when the gate suddenly opened and a 'black maria' came out. It turned sharp left and I saw the back window was open and I could hear men calling to me. There was nobody else about at the time, and when I went back to my room I told my roommates what had happened. Next morning we heard the tragic news that eight men had been taken to Big Wave Bay and executed. They were mostly connected with the Hong Kong and Shanghai Bank and one of them had been a great friend of ours in Chefoo, namely Ginger Hyde. Had he recognized me and were they trying to give me a message? I was too far away to hear what they said. Later his wife Eileen died in camp leaving a six-year-old son. Another man in the 'black maria' was the American husband of Elsie Soares, the Portugese girl I had stayed the night with, during the fighting. I heard that Elsie had married him after the surrender — much later I heard that she had had a baby and that she had been badly tortured in the Hong Kong gaol when the Japanese tried to obtain information about her husband's activities. I was told by somebody who saw her afterwards that she looked like an old lady. I hope the years have brought her peace.

The needs in our lives were many. Our clothes were strange and very varied and often most ingenious. At one point in the early days, an issue of different brands of flour came into camp in cotton bags. The material was nice and soft when washed and cool to wear. I got enough flour bags to make a pair of short pyjamas. I had one brand on my top half, with grapes on one leg and swallows on the other and these lasted me for 3½ years and were much admired! A blackout curtain that I had looted made me quite a smart two piece swim suit — so I was able to bathe when the Japanese opened Tweed Bay at certain times for us. This was a beautiful small bay to swim in. The Japanese had floating drums to mark where we could swim out to. If we went beyond this, a rifle shot soon warned us. After the war we heard that one of the young policemen had been attacked and killed by a shark while swimming there. If I had known that there was a likelihood of sharks I would never have swum out as far as the drums.

Later we got an issue of a thick khaki 'jumper'. These were square and sleeveless with a V neck and seam down the sides. Some people wore them as they were, but if one was fortunate to get two, there was enough material to make a pair of warm slacks. With the odd bits of leftovers I made mittens and embroidered bookmarkers for presents and other small items. One of the Russian Hong Kong policemen got two jumpers and evidently thought my slacks looked all right, so he asked if I could make him a pair of trousers — the first and the last pair of men's trousers that I have ever made. They were a great success and he showed his gratitude by bringing me some much coveted carrots he had grown in a small patch of ground outside his room.

Needles and thread were not easily come by — they were worth their weight in gold. There was only one sewing machine and only those who had brought in sewing material had any to share with others, so it was all very precious. Our woollen cardigans were unravelled and reknitted many times. We were fast running out of all the necessities of life such as soap; toothpaste (replaced with lye, an ash from the kitchen fires); toilet paper was virtually unobtainable, very occasionally an issue of terrible paper could be bought at the canteen; for writing material we used Chinese cigarette packets opened out to draft our letters home as we could not afford to make a mistake on the official card the Japanese so seldom gave us; medicines were practically nil, even at the hopital; fuel was running out and we had used all our doors except the one to the washroom. We had no floorboards like some of the flats, because our floors were cement and sometimes the men who built and 'manned' the coppers that gave us a hot drink in the morning had only grass to use which gave off a heavy smoke. It was terrible for them and for those at the head of the queue.

For those who smoked, life was very hard. The craving was so great that they smoked dried tea leaves, sweet potato leaves etc. — all re-collected as butt-ends and re-smoked rolled into any piece of paper that could be found. The extreme suffering that was caused made me realize years ago what a terrible hold this drug tobacco has on people. No one realizes how difficult it is to give up until they are forced to go without, and many risks were taken to get cigarettes and sell them again for food.

Much has been written about the rations in Japanese prison camps. Four ounces of cooked rice and a ladle of vegetable stew — mostly rotten lettuce or chives — does not do much for one when one is hungry. We had a few ounces of meat at the beginning but none for the final 18 months. We had a small ration of flour at first, but this ended when the Americans left. Salt was hard to get and often very dirty, mixed with hairs and stones so that one had to wash it and use the liquid, allowing the dirt to sink first. When salt ran out altogether we were allowed to cook the rice in seawater, as stomach cramps had started with some people. Our sugar ration was about one tablespoon a week and this adds no flavour to boiled rice. Rice water was kept for dysentery patients and bran was sent to the clinic for sufferers of beri beri. This had to be wetted down so that it could not be sold by those to whom it was given. The only tasty meal I had was one stolen from the kitchen garbage can! Two of us took the can out on to a hill and sorted every speck of edible material, mostly the size of your thumbnail (and believe me there was not much that the kitchen left).

I understand that we were supposed to get one Red Cross parcel every two weeks. I got four and a half parcels in three and a half years, some American and some English. Strangely the most satisfying dish for me was a tin of rice milk pudding packed in Devonshire and beautifully creamy — seems unbelievable after a diet of so little except tasteless rice. Only those who know what hunger is can understand how much those parcels meant to us. The terrible feeling that there was just nothing to eat, and the hunger pains that came after months of semi-starvation have to be experienced to be believed. I could get no satisfaction by thinking "How lovely a good hunk of fruit cake would be". I realized it was too dangerous and too easy to let oneself dwell on the thought and become almost mental thinking of food.

Towards the end a ration of fish paste was given to us. The smell and taste was terrible, but I discovered that if I put the fish paste on the tip of my spoon with some rice behind it, I could get it down quite well. Although very objectionable, this fish was not rotten, but in fact, very nutritious. Those who could not stomach it passed it on to me and I was most grateful for the extra rations and really did quite well!

We became ingenious in trying to give some change to our very tasteless diet. We cooked sweet potato leaves, marrow leaves, pumpkin flowers, banana skins (when available), porridge (when we had a canteen and sufficient money and spare coupons). The porridge had to be heated on a pan so that the weevils were killed first, they used to pop up and the whole thing appeared alive. Nell Hale swore she would never touch porridge again. I wonder if she has kept her vow?

This confined life and near-starvation diet was too much for the well-known figure of General Frank ('One-Armed') Sutton R.E. He was an exceptionally large man with a superb physique and had an amazing capacity mentally and physically as I had learnt from meeting him pre-war and reading a book he lent me, written by himself, about his amazing life in China as a general in Marshall Chang Tso-Lin's army in the 1920s. I was to meet him again under sadder circumstances when we were both prisoners at Stanley.

He had lost his right arm in 1915, when serving with the Royal Engineers at Gallipoli. He bravely picked up four Turkish hand-grenades as they fell into a trench but the fifth exploded before he could throw it clear.

He was a great sportsman, and (rather incongruously) had taken his golf-clubs to Gallipoli. It seemed this tragedy would be the end of sport for him, but being the determined and energetic man that he was, it just meant that he learned to play left-handed and remained a top player.

He used to walk the perimeter of the camp dressed in shorts and his familiar towelling jacket and always swinging a golf-club. His large frame could not survive the hunger and strain of those days and this dynamic personality, who had once armed and led his Chinese troops with many of their weapons invented by himself, died in Stanley Camp.

While Frank Sutton had backed a northern warlord, another well-known China personality from Britain had backed the southern leader Dr. Sun Yat-Sen and became his bodyguard. General Morris Abraham Cohen, or 'Two-Gun-Cohen' as he was always referred to, because of the two Colt .44 revolvers he carried in his belt in tooled leather holsters was also sent to Stanley. At one time he was an interpreter of Cantonese in the law courts of Alberta, Canada, helping Chinese who had suffered under foreign oppression in the same way as his own Hebrew people, and later he was a Sergeant-Major in the Canadian Marines. He was a London Cockney Jew, born in Stepney in 1889 the eldest son of Jewish immigrants from Poland; a perfect man for the part of 'bodyguard' with his battered prize-fighter face.

He first met Dr. Sun Yat-Sen in Canada and later in China became a close friend of the family. He was instrumental in helping Mme. Sun and her sister Mrs. Kung (two of the famous Sung sisters, the third being Mme. Chiang Kai-Shek) escape from Hong Kong the day before the installations were destroyed by the R.A.F. and Kai Tak was evacuated. Mme. Sun had constantly refused to go, saying: "If there is fighting here there will be wounded, and refugees and children will suffer. Perhaps I may be able to help them. I shall stay right here." Morris Cohen played his last card explaining to her that she was a national hero, and if she stayed while the fortress fell, a lot of Chinese would take arms to defend her and she would be the cause of many unnecessary deaths. Mme. Sun appreciated that point and left as soon as there was a plane available.

'Two-Gun' Cohen was caught in Hong Kong in 1941 and was very badly treated by the Japanese. They had hoped to get a great deal of information from a man with such a colourful background and so many important contacts. Only his strength of will, courage and wisdom enabled him to come through such an ordeal. Eventually the Japanese sent him to Stanley camp where he rested and recovered and was later repatriated with the Canadians when they left on the *'Teia Maru'* for their exchange at Goa so he did not suffer the sad fate of 'One-Armed' Sutton.

In September 1944, we had a great scare about the water situation — whether we would be rationed. The Japanese announced that owing to the shortage of coal, water could not be pumped to the filter beds for distribution and there would be water from the taps for four hours only one day in five. A well was opened in the oval opposite our block and we had to queue block by block and room by room for our small ration of water. Suitable containers to collect and store water was quite a problem. At specific times we were allowed to collect sea water from the beach close by for use in the toilets. This was a great help and avoided having to use latrines, but it was a very exhausting job carrying as much water as one could up from the beach. This went on for some time and how the problem was solved I cannot remember, but eventually we returned to normal. Probably a ship came from Japan with coal.

One night we were in bed and carrying on a whispered conversation, as we were not allowed to talk after dark, when a Japanese guard heard us and shouted from below. We stopped at once and thought all was well but we suddenly realized he had come up the stairs and was standing at the entrance to our room trying unsuccessfully to find the light switch. He was at the foot of my bed and one could almost hear everyone holding their breath and wondering what would happen. Much to the relief of all he decided to give up, turned round, and left. The light switch was at the head of my bed by the communicating door and we were glad he had not continued his search.

Our activities varied as our strength deteriorated. There were many talented people who willingly gave of their talents. In the early days a ballet dancer gave classes for those interested. I found it very good to do a few mild exercises to music while I had the energy, but that did not last long. We were very fortunate that the Americans had been able to bring in their club library and when they were repatriated they

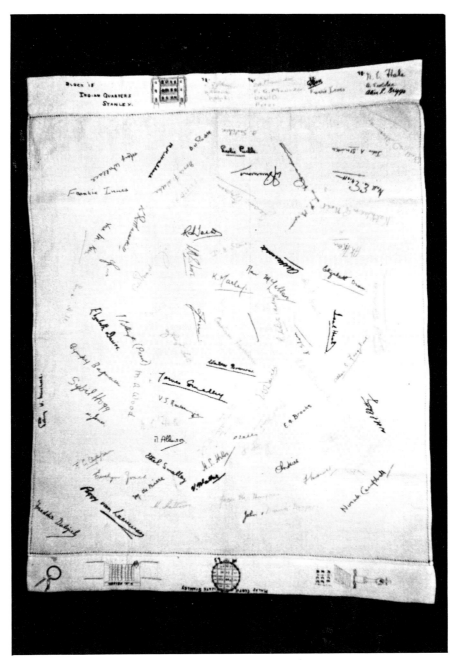

The full cloth with signatures. Top L-R Block 13 and flat signatures.
Bottom R-L: Steps up to clock giving mealtime and rice below steps — Centre
Malay Certificate — Jail Gates with Japanese guard — far L. ring of 10 cent
piece.

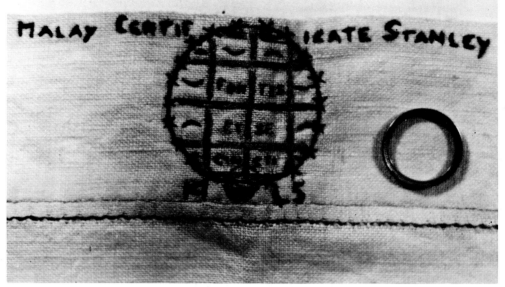

Malay Certificate worked on same linen square — also ring punched from 10 cent piece and worn by author in camp.

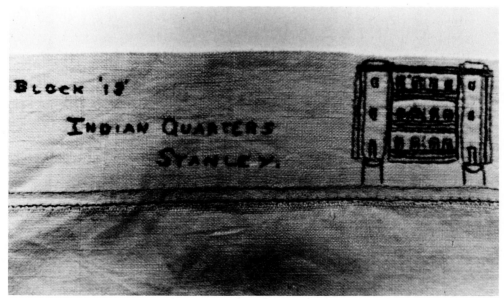

Worked by author on piece of 'looted' linen made into square for internee's signatures. Section of Block 13 — author's 'flat' — L. stairway centre floor.

left it with us. There were many excellent books which were much enjoyed.

We also had concerts and plays of quite high standard and some amazingly good productions such as 'Private Lives' by Noel Coward and many others. Considering the difficulties and lack of commodities these productions were ingenious and quite remarkable. We always had to get permission beforehand to produce anything, but the Japanese used to attend and seemed to enjoy the performances. The only thing they would not allow was dancing - it was stopped in the very early days.

We could attend classes in French or Malay. The students of Malay were given a 'certificate' at the end of their course which was designed in Stanley Camp and presented at the completion of their studies. The emblem is a circle of barbed wire round squares of iron bars in the centre — in the six centre squares is written FONTES ETSE CINCTI (Although our sources of knowledge are encircled.). A blue wavy line depicts the sea. At the bottom of the circle of barbed wire is a padlock. These were issued to the students in 1945. I embroidered this certificate onto a piece of linen along with many of the internees names.

I studied French for a while, a group of us would find a spot on the hillside and the French Consul was our teacher. I was amazed how much of my 'school French' came back to me. I enjoyed this very much but found that I had to give it up as trying to concentrate was keeping me from sleeping. This happened to many who tried to study. It was a very great strain trying to study on an empty stomach. We had University professors in camp who tutored people who wanted to matriculate. I understand that those who did matriculate were recognized after the war.

We had no electricity in the evenings except in the early days, so we organized 'talks' in each others rooms in the winter. Something I used to love listening to on a summer evening was the police choir. There were a number of White Russians in the choir and their singing was truly lovely. These Russians were descendants of the Russians who fled to China in the 1920s at the time of the revolution. I was very impressed at the tidiness and homeliness that these men achieved with the small corner (just a bed space) that was their 'home'. They made surroundings as attractive as possible — hanging a bright piece of material or picture on their space of wall above their bed. It was not everybody who had this capacity to keep up morale but it helped a great deal if one could. Another instance of this was a Dutch mother with three children who made a point of trying to help them to grow up knowing how to behave. She used a piece of material as a tablecloth on an upturned box which she set with what utensils she had for their meagre meal so that the children would not find life too strange when they were freed.

I find it difficult to write about our 'daily chores'; they varied from block to block and the circumstances one lived in. I have mentioned earlier the different types of accommodation. I lived in what we called the 'Indian Block' which housed the Indian warders and their families pre-war. There were seven blocks, three-storeys high, each side of the oval. The Hong Kong police were in one block and we were fortunate to have them manning our communal kitchen.

The Japanese liked to keep us on Tokyo time which meant that often we had to get up while the moon was still shining or it was still dark to collect our ration of boiling water to make a cup of tea. We often stood for ages in the dark and cold while the poor fire-stoker tried to get the water boiling on grass while he was suffocated by smoke. If ones' container was large you might be lucky in getting a little extra water, and sad was the day that I slipped on the wet grassy bank with my bare feet and broke my large 'looted' Chinese teapot and I was back again to my army water bottle. Tea was precious and bought in the canteen when there was one; it must have been the sweepings as it consisted of twigs and all sorts of odd-looking bits.

We had our small bed area to keep tidy and shared the cleaning of the toilet and the kitchen. If there was a canteen, roll-call, or anything special to collect, our block supervisor would call out and we took our turn in the queue. At about 10 a.m. we had to queue for the mid-day meal (such as it was) and at 5 p.m. we queued again — our only two meals of the day.

Everything issued had to be queued for, sometimes taking up much of one's day. We always said our life was "All pees and queues" because an almost total rice diet had that effect on one. The weaker we got the less time we had to spare — everything took us so much longer to achieve.

I think most situations in life have a humourous side even an internment camp was no exception and we tried to make the most of this aspect.

At one time we had Indian guards during the day and there was one who used to parade up and down looking into our room which was level with a bank at the back, so he had a good view. We got concerned about this and before going to bed we jammed Nell's chair up against the handle of our verandah door (before it was used for firewood). We had all settled into bed when we heard a grating noise on the cement floor. Nell spoke a little Hindustani so up she leapt to do battle and flung open the door to find a terrified Chinese policeman (not the Indian)! His stockings were stuffed with cigarettes for re-sale to internees but he had come to the wrong block. Everybody, including the young Chinese, was very relieved.

Quite frequently we had a roll-call, which meant that the personnel in each block had to stand to attention in front of their blocks while a Japanese officer walked past, wearing white gloves and with a very long sword clanking along the ground at his side. One day the order came that we must bow as he passed. When he passed us we all dutifully bowed feeling complete fools — and apparently looking so — because from across the oval we heard a faint ripple of mirth from the block on the opposite side where the occupants had a back view of us! We must have looked quite extraordinary, men, women and children, all shapes and sizes dressed in their odd apparel. However, the mirth was sternly stamped on. The Japanese officer was furious and made the offenders stand for an hour in the hot sun. We all felt very sad for them.

A lot has been written about the atrocities and hardships suffered by prisoners of the Japanese. I know that they are true and I condemn such brutalities in any nation or person, they are hurtful to even think about. I also know that there are two sides to every coin. I would like to write about a few instances that were "Kindnesses" and present the other side of the coin.

On the ground floor below my room lived some nursing sisters from the Matilda Hospital. One of them had a birthday and her room-mates had saved a little here and a little there to make her a birthday cake with the usual rice flour flavoured with chopped banana skins. The cake was duly cooked and put on their kitchen slab waiting the happy occasion. In the meantime, an Alsatian belonging to one of the Japanese guards found the kitchen and ate the cake. He must have been hungry, like us. You can imagine the distress to the Sisters that this caused and we all felt very sorry for them. Somehow, the Japanese officers at H.Q. heard of this tragedy and next day the nurses received a box of Chinese cakes and everyone was happy.

A Mrs. Kerr, who spoke and wrote Japanese, was always willing to help when a translation was needed. I had not heard any news of Patricia for a year so I asked Mrs. Kerr if she would come with me to the Japanese Headquarters to see if there was any way of finding out about her. She came with me willingly and I was told by the Japanese officer that if my letter cards were written in Japanese and I signed them they would get through, and they did. I was overjoyed to receive quite a long typed letter from Patricia in English with her signature at the end — you can imagine how excited and grateful I was. It was written from Baguio on 13th December, 1943 and I received it on Easter Sunday 9th April 1944 — quite quick for those days. In part she says "My height is 5ft, weight 74½lb. My hair is short and I have a braid on one side with a red streak in front. I am in 6th grade and doing well". Some of the things I was so anxious to hear.

Another kindness to me personally concerned a photograph of Christopher. I had no photo or snap of him with me. He had a photo taken, in naval uniform, just before I was evacuated from Hong Kong to Sydney. It had been taken by a Japanese photographer who had a shop in the arcade of the Hong Kong Hotel and who I reckoned would still be in business. So I asked Mrs. Kerr if she would come with me to headquarters again and ask if the Japanese officer could get a copy for me. He seemed very keen to do this and I gave him all particulars, hoping for the best. In a few days, I was overjoyed to receive a postcard size copy of the photograph, which I still have.

A Japanese soldier used to swagger into the camp in the late afternoon with his hands in his pockets, he just seemed to be wandering around, but very soon we noticed a lot of small children following him, so we nicknamed him the 'Pied Piper'. We discovered that he stuffed his trouser pockets full of sweets of some kind to disburse to them and they must have been the first sweets that many of the younger ones had ever seen.

As I said before, there are 'two sides to every coin'. It is fortunate for the world that this is so. We are not meant to forget but we are meant to forgive. War can bring out the worst or the best in human nature, whatever the nationality. It was present in our own community with the stresses of everyday living in Stanley.

Many years after the war I met an Indian man who was a manager in Air-India and had spent some years in Japan. He was telling me of the many different ways the Japanese have of addressing different people in society and the most polite way was always used when addressing children. I was very interested to hear this because Japanese children always speak so respectfully to their elders and have polite manners. I feel we could learn a lot from this revelation. Chinese children also have this pleasant and respectful attitude towards their elders which stands them in good stead for their place in society. They

Christopher. The photo I had in camp.

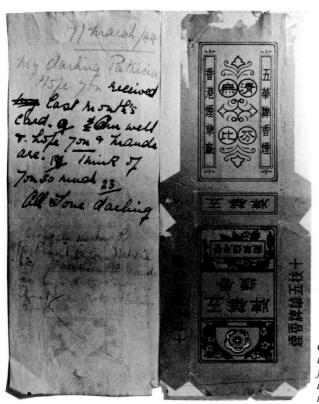

Cigarette packet used to draft notes to family. Faded writing is Japanese translation.

IMPERIAL JAPANESE ARMY

1. I am interned at Philippine Internment Camp No. ____1____

2. My health is — ~~excellent~~: good; ~~fair; poor.~~

3. Message. (Limited to 25 words.)

Dear Mummy: Cards January, February received

Three from Ducher. Height 5ft 1". Weight 84.

Live Mat Shed. Doing well school. We grow

beans, onions, greens. Love

Sept. 6, 1944   *Patricia Briggs*
                              Signature

The type of card received from Patricia at Santa Tomas. 'Ducher' is what she always called her grandmother at that time.

learn it from the way they are addressed by their parents.

The types of Japanese enlisted towards the end of the war were very superior to the earlier enlistments who were mostly from the uneducated country communities. Later they came from academic and educated levels, and at this time orders were given to all troops that the ignominious face-slapping be stopped. In all honesty, I cannot say that I hated or feared the Japanese — I hated what they did to so many during World War II and conversely I hate what has been done by so many of my own and other nationals. Many people will not like my saying this but I want to look at it fairly from both sides. I think if you read back in history — even as recently as the convict settlement of this country — Australia — where I now live, one must admit that we have done many terrible things, even to our own people, that we would dearly like to forget. If history is truthfully written, they will never be forgotten — but I sincerely hope they may be forgiven though this is harder than to forgive wartime atrocities. War is hurtful to all concerned directly and indirectly and in many ways, but brutalities in peacetime are surely unforgiveable.

Some years after the war I heard a Japanese woman who was a socialist senator accept responsibility, as a woman, for the way her country's menfolk had behaved during the war — something they did not hear about in Japan until all the stories came out at the end of the war. It must have been very hard to believe. When Mr. Nobosuke Kishi was the liberal prime minister of Japan (about 1958), he decided he would go on a goodwill and trade mission throughout Southeast Asia and Australia. The socialist senator heard of this and she was most concerned. She had been to Asia after the war and knew the reception that Mr. Kishi would receive. However, she had the courage to go and see him and said "Your tour will be a failure unless you go on a tour of reconciliation". He accepted her advice and courageously went to Southeast Asia and Australia with this message and perhaps the most courageous thing he did was to go back to his own parliament and tell them what he had done.

Much water has run under the bridge between Japan and Australia since then. Beliefs and inhibitions go very deep into our past — our ancient cultures and customs are so very different and yet Christopher and I have felt there is an empathy between Japan and Britain — we both come from old feudal systems, both are surrounded by sea and both are seagoing nations — and living in China we found that when the 'twain' did meet, the result was a very capable and energetic mixture.

I have been reading a book called 'Prisoner of the British' by Professor Yuji Aida of the University of Kyoto and I found this very interesting. He speaks of the 'mental cruelty' of the British when he was a prisoner in Burma from the end of the war until May 1947.

Looking at his attitude from his point of view also from my own, I feel both the Japanese and the British are a proud people and possibly some of the feelings towards others stem very simply from just 'conceit'.

The British arrogance and sense of superiority generally speaking is more marked when dealing with strangers or foreigners than with their own people. This is the same with the Japanese. Is it a self-defence or a desire to make a good impression? I think much of Professor Aida's feelings may come from the fact that he is an academic and that the stresses and hardships of war were something he only knew of from an academic background and the reality of it all was a very hard thing for him to take, coupled with the fact that a Japanese of his class would consider himself superior to a Westerner anyway. I agree with Mr. Louis Allen, who helped translate Professor Aida's book, that if Professor Aida was to visit the British Isles with an open mind, hopefully he would acquire a different view by meeting people on their home ground.

I was fortunate to have met and been friendly with some senior Japanese in China before the war, which I am sure helped me greatly to realize that all Japanese were not "tarred with the same brush", any more than all Englishmen.

About August 1945 I was sorry to see my friends Gympy and Theo Bagram leave the camp. Nobody knew the reason — only that various technicians had orders to be ready to leave with their wives and families for an 'unknown destination' at 2.30 p.m. Baggage parties were called for and all was ready — but no sign of the launch that they were to board. It eventually arrived and they finally got on board at 3 a.m. How tired they must all have been — the launch was small with nowhere to sleep and no toilet facilities. I went to farewell the Bagrams. Theo was on a hospital stretcher as he was unable to walk — he had propped himself up on one elbow and looked rather like a Roman aristocrat lying on a couch. Both were as cheerful as ever — a wonderful couple. Their 'destination' is still unknown to me as I write, but I hope whatever was in front of them was not too hard and they did not suffer too much.

On January 16th, 1945 there was a very sad and unhappy incident at St. Stephens College. The Japanese had a mobile anti-aircraft gun on the road to the fort which ran below the bungalows, and our (allied) planes were trying to hit it, but the bomb unfortunately fell near the bungalows killing fourteen internees.

In early August 1945 rumours were rife and it was hard to know what to believe. One felt that things were happening in the world that we had no conception of — and that some change was coming into our lives. It was very heartening, but when we really knew the truth that we were about to be free men and women again, our minds just could not take it in. The camp was quiet and if there was any rowdy rejoicing it did not come my way. We had lost our security for the second time and the numbness that we felt when we surrendered to the Japanese three years and eight months ago came back to us again and we were much weaker to cope with the trauma. I find it hard to recall those days, perhaps because they seemed so blank at the time, but I have before me a copy of the *"South China Morning Post"* dated Saturday September 1st, 1945, which I would like to quote from in part; giving a clearer picture than we knew of what was happening at that time:-

"SURRENDER SCENE, LONG AND DREARY WAIT"
"For three weeks since Japan's surrender Hong Kong residents have been looking forward to the change of regimes, waiting patiently for the arrival in the harbour of the fleet which was known to be somewhere near. On Thursday (August 30th) the dreary waiting ended . . . The first talk of definite peace came on Saturday August 11th when we heard the preliminary announcement quoting a 'Domei' message that the Japanese government had agreed to accept the Potsdam Peace Declaration. The bare message instantly became magnified beyond all proportion — 'Japanese Government's capitulation had been confirmed by signature' — rumour's giving hours on Friday or Saturday as the time for signing — 'planes expected to demonstrate over the Colony on Saturday afternoon' — 'Allied delegates said to be on their way to Hong Kong by sea, land and air with Sunday as the probable date for change over' . . . As the hours dragged monotonously on, Wednesday brought a more hopeful atmosphere when it became known that the Emperor of Japan was to broadcast an important announcement . . . Five minutes before the appointed hour an unusually large crowd began to assemble . . . at De Voeux Road and Pedder Street intersection to hear the studio's relay from Tokyo. Japanese nationals, civilian and military predominated, solemn, pensive, despondent. Among the

*waiting hundreds were many Chinese parasites — realizing their
innings were fast running out — on the off chance of hearing
an English interpretation of the broadcast. The Japanese National
Anthem was played, the Japanese standing rigidly to attention.
In a strong voice that seemed choked with sobs, the Emperor
spoke . . . he did not use the words 'surrender' or 'capitulation'
he spoke of compromise peace and appealed to the loyalty of
his subjects . . . to cultivate the ways of rectitude, foster nobili-
ty of spirit and work with resolution so that they may enhance
the innate glory of the Imperial State and keep pace with the progress of the world.*

*At the conclusion of what was described as a masterpiece of
oratory, the Japanese anthem was again played . . . Following
this authentic confirmation of Japan's defeat, the Colony waited
impatiently for the changeover. Rumours of the release of certain government officials from Stanley seemed to bring victory
day near . . . Saturday August 18th brought more gratifying happenings when it became known that the camps (prisoners of war
at Kowloon, internees at Stanley), had been thrown open to the
public . . . In town the community's hopes were so keyed up that
celebrations began on Saturday 18th August when the Chinese
colours were hoisted and crackers fired. Large flags were selling
at Y3,000 each . . . but the Japanese authorities took exception
to this premature display and ordered all flags to be lowered.
Still the days dragged on. People . . . were now restless in having to wait a few more days and felt cheated of their part in the
world wide relief and celebrations. Now at least the navy is here
and it is all over. So Desu!!''*

On Thurday 30th August a very moving ceremony took place at
Stanley. We heard someone calling out "The Navy is here", and we
all rushed up to what we called 'The married block' which was the
centre of the camp with a fairly big open space. There, for the first
time we saw our own navy — officially signalling the restoration of
British control of Hong Kong. There the Union Jack was again un-
furled with the flags of allied nations and we were addressed by Rear
Admiral Harcourt. That evening the admiral broadcast messages from
His Majesty, the secretary of state for the Colonies, and himself, to
the people of Hong Kong. Unfortunately only those with radios were
able to hear it direct. His Majesty's long and loving message showed
his feeling towards us and in part His Majesty said — "The thoughts
of the Queen and myself have been constantly with you during your

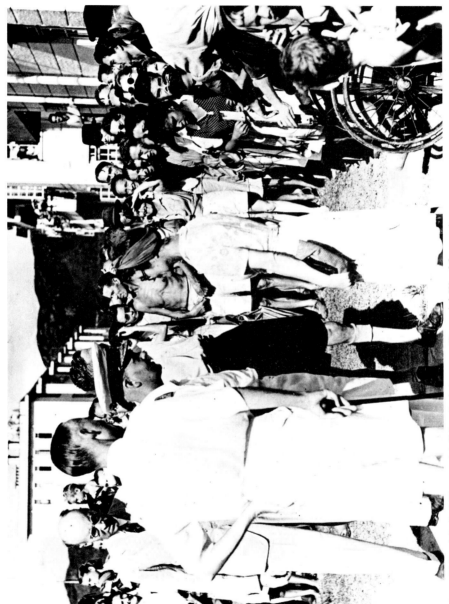

Aug. 1945. Admiral Harcourt talking to internees. (Imperial War Museum)

Aug. 1945. Flag raising ceremony outside 'married' block Stanley Camp. (photo Imperial War Museum)

years of suffering so bravely borne and, in the dawn of the days of liberation, we rejoice with you that the ties which united my people everywhere will now be fully restored. The thoughts of the Queen and myself have been constantly with you . . . I know full well that these ties of loyalty and affection between myself and my far eastern peoples have never been broken, but they have been maintained in darkness and in suffering. The time has come when their strength and permanence will again be displayed in triumph before the whole world.'' The whole text of His Majesty's message was printed for all to see in the *"South China Morning Post"* of 1st September 1945.

Some of the husbands and friends who had been in Shamshui Po camp were now allowed into Stanley — many were unable to stand for long from weakness, others were partially blind from malnutrition as were some in our own camp. The police and government officials were the first to go back into Hong Kong. The changeover was wonderfully achieved. A very difficult operation that, if not planned to the last detail, could have meant our annihilation. I heard after, that this had been planned by the Japanese for August anyway as they were unable to feed their own people much longer. The short rations in Japan were being severely felt.

A number of people gradually returned to Hong Kong, some to catch up with the threads of their businesses or homes or to find out who was left or how much damage was done — to try and recapture their lives that had been wrenched apart so suddenly and remorselessly. Some have been able to do this but I fear that there were many whose lives were disrupted and broken forever.

One day I was told that two naval officers wanted to see me and wondering who they were I went to greet them. They were two Australians who had met Christopher in Bombay and knew that I was at Stanley. I wish I could remember their names. They were my first contact with the outside world for 3 ½ years and it meant a great deal to me. They were anxious to see something of the camp and I took them round but when it came to any hill they both had to take my hands to help me up. It was quite a while since I had walked so far and had not realized how weak I had become.

A very odd thing happened to my camp bed that last week. It had stood up wonderfully for 3 ½ years being my only support as a bed or place to sit. I had kept it free of bugs by some miracle until they claimed it at the very last and I had a few miserable nights — then the day I was leaving it suddenly ripped right down the middle where my name had been painted — as much as to say ''I have supported you proudly and loyally and now I am finished, farewell''!

And so it was 'farewell' with no regrets but still this awful uncertainty and wondering 'What next? Where and what does the future hold?' Knowing in one's heart that the difficulties would be great — perhaps greater than one could manage — that things would never be the same — but I hoped for courage, and felt great gratitude that I was given strength to reach the end and be alive as there were many we had to leave behind forever.

When at the age of 17, I was staying for a short period with my grandmother and Aunt Lina in a flat in Hampstead, a friend of theirs came to visit who was quite good at 'reading' hands, and for fun she offered to read mine. She told me much that has proved correct over the years — "You will never be rich but you will never be in want. etc. etc." She then puzzled for a while and said "You will travel to a country very far away — and you seem to be shut up — but I can't see it clearly". It meant nothing to me at the time. When I was in internment camp I met a man who had had his fortune told by a friend in Hong Kong before the war and he was told "If I did not know you well I would say you are going to be locked up or going to gaol". Coincidence — or insight of what was to come?

I was not anxious to join the others in going into Hong Kong and perhaps seeing the destruction in my home as I felt pretty sure it had been looted by the Chinese the night before the Japanese arrived. However, I heard from a friend who did go to Kowloon and who visited my flat that there was nothing of ours there — the furniture was all different and it had been occupied by Japanese officers.

We lived with constant rumours in those first days of freedom. "When were we leaving? Where would be our port of call? and Would we all be able to go? All the answers were different, of course.

I quote again from the *'South China Morning Post'* of 1st September 1945 from the leading article:-

> *"Forty-four lost months of our lives, a thousand or more dreary days and nights of waiting and hoping, starving, praying and enduring. Only buried alive, conscious of great tumult far off wherein we could have been participating . . . Now for us, the forgotten folk, life begins again. We return to the world . . . Some are not with us, will not awaken again . . . And we, who by the grace of God survived, emerge from entombment, leaner, prematurely aged and spiritually very tired, to justify our existence anew, to try to overtake the march of time . . . History has moved far on, left us stumbling an age behind . . . With the end of a*

difficult war, more difficulties begin to construct a new world order, to secure the general acceptance of the truth that war will only cease when the causes of war have been destroyed. Are we equal to it?"

To me 'spiritually very tired' and 'to try to overtake the march of time' were very much key points. There was so much to take in, there were so many 'words', 'names' and 'incidents' we never heard of before the war, which with normal health would have just left us confused but with the proverbial 'camp tiredness' at times it seemed well nigh impossible. Feelings of inferiority were experienced when people laughed and you did not understand what they were laughing about. Anybody who has been through a similar experience will, I think, understand what I mean. The 'tiredness' one seemed to have no control over and it came on so suddenly. I read of a motor accident in which a man who had been a prisoner was involved. The doctor giving evidence referred to the condition as 'camp tiredness'. I remember when an aunt took Patricia and me to Hampton Court soon after our return to England a longing came over me to just lie down on the gravel path — anywhere — not minding about the people around me. The condition wore off to a great extent as my health gradually improved.

By early September people were beginning to disperse from the camp and then the great event was forecast and we began to collect our meagre belongings. I still had my small suitcase and was given a tin deed-box by my room-mate Nell Hale, and in these I packed all my worldly goods.

Chapter 7

HOMEWARD BOUND

On the 9th September 1945, the first parties boarded the *S.S. 'Empress of Australia'* from Queens Pier, which then sailed round the islands to Stanley to pick up the civilian internees. And so we left Stanley with no regrets and went on board at 4.30 p.m. on 10th September, 1945. She had accommodation for a thousand repatriates and was very crowded. She was the last remaining liner of the *'Empress'* ships. The food was something we had not tasted for a long time, very welcome but quite the wrong kind for us, such as dehydrated potatoes, and very soon I had beri-beri and could feel my legs swelling as I sat at the table, it was most uncomfortable. In camp I had the 'dry' type of beri-beri with aching joints and was given a ration of bran which helped to relieve the condition. But now I had the 'wet' type with swelling of the tissues.

Our destination was unknown when we left Hong Kong — perhaps India — perhaps Australia — perhaps U.K.? We called at Manila to pick up P.O.W's coming from Japan and Korea where they had been taken from Singapore and Hong Kong. Many prisoners had never reached their destination as some ships were torpedoed en route to Japan. I knew that my brother had been sent to Korea from Changi so I used to meet each boat load as they came on board to ask the men if they had met 'Bill Murray'. Eventually I spoke to a man called Patrick Crawshaw, Royal Engineers, who had been in Changi. He said he had taught German in camp to my cousin (Kenneth) Brig. K.S. Crawford, also Royal Engineers, and a cousin of his, whose name he did not know. Until then I had no idea Kenneth had been prisoner (for the second time in his life, as he was a prisoner during the siege of Kut in World War I). As a senior officer the Japanese had sent him to Mukden. I continued my enquiries with no luck.

One morning my flatmate Pat Fox and I were leaning over the ship's rail when we spotted an American frigate steaming into port. There were a number of men on the high bridge and one was looking towards us through binoculars. I said to Pat "Those men are not American, I can tell by the way they stand", — we agreed on that point and went down to lunch. I then went to my cabin, there was a knock on the door and I said "Come in" and in walked my brother! He was the man on the frigate who had been looking through the binoculars trying to see if he could spot me on board. When he arrived at the P.O.W. transit camp he met a naval man from Hong Kong and asked if he knew me and he replied "I was talking to her this morning". Bill broke camp — borrowed a jeep and came down to the ship. It was the most marvellous meeting and I was glad how well he looked considering all things. Korea is a much healthier climate and Bill and Kenneth were fortunate in leaving the hardships and the climate of Malaysia or the Burma Railway. Bill was sent to England via America so we did not meet again until I got home in October. When Kenneth was to leave Mukden he overslept and missed his plane so had to leave on a later one. Unfortunately all his luggage went on the first plane and he eventually was met in Manila by Bill, still wearing his pyjamas! Patrick Crawshaw was most upset when I introduced him to Bill and he realized the 'cousin' he had taught was in fact my brother about whom I had been enquiring.

The first thing I did when I got to Manila was to try and find out news of Patricia, hoping I might meet up with her there. I was told she had already left, via America, which was a great disappointment. However, it was a relief to know she was safe and had gone straight to England with Christopher's cousin with whom she had been during the war. Manila had surrendered some months before Hong Kong and the Americans had repatriated all the internees immediately. So we were not to meet until October in England and I had so hoped to be home for her birthday.

The events in the Philippines were something I knew nothing about till after the war. I knew that Patricia, then aged 9½, with Stephen and Maude Crawfurd had gone to Baguio, 5-6 thousand feet up in the mountains and approximately 100 miles from Manila. It was the summer capital of the Philippines, and hoped they would be safer there than in Manila.

Patricia in her own words recaptures some of the events that she remembers of that time:-

"We were spending our Christmas holidays at Baguio in December 1941 when the Japanese arrived in the Philippines. Several weeks later when their arrival in Baguio was imminent we all gathered at Brent School.

135

We had brought our few personal belongings as we were pretty sure that we would not be returning home again. The first Japanese soldiers we saw arrived at Brent School in a small yellow taxi. Stephen by this time had returned to Manila as he had business responsibilities to attend to. This left Maude and me to look after each other for the next two years.

From Brent School we walked to the army barracks — camp John Hay — carrying our possessions. This was quite a walk and not much fun carrying bags, etc., but a kindly friend helped to carry ours, we must have looked a sorry pair.

The barracks consisted of one double and one single-storey building. The double-storey had sleeping quarters upstairs and the dining kitchen area downstairs. Men and women were separated for sleeping and the women and children were in the single storey building. We had bunk beds with horsehair mattresses and not much living space. This was over compensated by plenty of room to move about outside. There were large playing fields opposite the barracks and at the start we were allowed to walk in the surrounding hillside. After several people had tried to escape, this luxury was no longer open to us.

In some ways we were lucky to be at Baguio, the climate was so much better than Manila, warm days and cold nights. The food was also plentiful. Rice was the basis of our diet — soft rice for breakfast — boiled rice for lunch and dinner. Luckily I loved rice and still do today. There was also a canteen where you could buy food. Maude used to sell her possessions to the Japanese guards in order to supplement our diet. The guards liked to buy jewellery, cameras and watches. We grew many of our own vegetables at the camp and slaughtered our own meat, so really we were well supplied with food in those first two years. The climate with its high rainfall was ideal for growing food. Fruit grew wild on the hills round the camp, and I can remember picking wild passion-fruit out on our walks.

There were 400 of us at Baguio and being a small group I am sure was to our advantage. Most people were on some sort of work team, because of course the internees did all the cooking, gardening, and maintenance of the camp. Maude was on a cook-team and supplemented our diet further with scraps from the kitchen, such as fish heads from which we made soup.

We were lucky to have a number of teachers with us in the camp, and all the children gathered for school each day. Our teachers were mission people and ran a very good little school. The teaching was in the American style as most of those living in the camp were Americans. We learnt in dollars and cents, so later, on the ship returning to England, Stephen had to teach me my sums using pounds, shillings, and pence. I have always been grateful to those teachers at Baguio for the time and effort they spent on us.

My closest friend at Baguio was a girl called Sally Ream who now lives in California. We were inseparable during this time and corresponded for many years after the war. Of course Sally and I would get up to all sorts of tricks as children always do. We used to love raiding the kitchens after they were closed and scrape the bottom of the rice cookers — this was lovely crisp boiled rice and delicious to eat. We used to like staying out late and playing games out on the playing fields. I was not allowed to stay out after a certain time and always got into serious trouble if I did. Sally and I used to play cribbage for hours at a time. Her father had a work-shop in the camp and made all sorts of things — wooden clogs to wear and dishes out of tin which we used for cooking. He was very handy and would make anything you wanted if he had the materials.

We seemed to keep very well in health. I had my appendix out during this time. There was a very good American doctor who took them out, and she was very proud of the result too as she kept saying she only used 2½ stitches for the wound! It was a proper little hospital, one that was already set up in the army barracks. I used to get the usual cold too frequently if I remember rightly, and Maude always kept me in bed for three days, a remedy that to this day I believe is the best treatment for a cold.

After two years in Baguio, Maude was allowed to join her husband in Manila. We travelled from Baguio, a distance of about 100 miles, in the back of a covered army truck. Our journey took us most of the day as the road winds and bends through very mountainous country. We had to stop frequently as people were continously being sick, the road was full of hairpin bends, a journey I will never forget. There were about 20 of us altogether. Amongst our party was a clergyman, and I can remember very well him singing and all of us joining in 'Home, Home, on the Range'. We were glad to reach Manila after a very hot and dusty journey.

There were 3700 people interned at Santa Thomas University.

It was a very different camp from the one we had just left. People were housed in the main university building and we started off there sleeping in a room with about 30 others. Soon after I arrived in Manila there was a measles epidemic and I promptly caught it. This put me in isolation for a couple of weeks.

After spending some months in the main building we were lucky enough to procure some building material to build ourselves a 'shanty'. These were one-room shacks made out of local material of bamboo and grass. Many people had their own 'shanties'. It meant that a husband could be with his wife and family. Of course it was so much nicer to be able to be a family unit instead of separated in the main buildings.

As in Baguio, everyone had jobs to do, such as caring for the people and maintenance for the camp. Stephen used to work in the vegetable garden, and later when he was too weak to work I used to tend his vegetable patch.

As the war drew on food became very scarce. Towards the end adults were only receiving 160 grams of cereal a day. By now many were suffering from lack of food. Towards the end of the third year as many as eight people a day were dying from starvation and others suffered badly from beri-beri. We were lucky to have a garden plot and so could supplement our meagre diet. The children were given extra rations, we had three meals a day while the grown-ups only had two.

By this time all schooling had stopped, people just did not have that sort of energy to keep going, it was all they could do to just exist and carry out the bare essentials of life.

I spent most of my time with three other girls, we were all very close and did everything together. Two of them had the same name as myself, so three out of four were called Pat. Several of them wanted to be ballet dancers, so long hours were spent doing handstands and cartwheels. We also liked to climb trees and spent hours on the swings. Our favourite way was for two to stand on the swings at the same time. On one of those occasions we both fell off and I came-to later after spending some time lying unconscious on the ground. It was during this time that I learnt how to knit and sew. I was very proud of the socks I knitted and of a blouse I made, all done by hand — no machines at that time. Also I had to spend time each day in reading, not a chore I liked as a child, I much preferred to be out climbing trees.

On the night of February 3rd 1945 American troops arrived at Santa Tomas and we were finally free once more, a day we had all been looking forward to for a long time. It was wonderful to see the American soldiers — they looked so huge to us for we had all shrunk in size and the Japanese soldiers were small in stature.

The Japanese guards took 200 of the internees as hostages. They were kept in one of the main buildings for 36 hours. During this time there were negotiations between the Japanese and Americans for their release. The Japanese wanted to be escorted back to their own lines in exchange for the hostages and this was agreed to by the Americans.

Our 'shanty' was next to the building which housed the hostages. One of the men tried to escape by climbing down a rope from the second story window but he slipped and broke his leg. He may have been in a weakened condition and not in a fit state to climb down a rope ladder. As our shanty was near where he fell we were able to help him into it and look after him till the crisis was over.

Three days after liberation the battle for Manila began. Santa Tomas was in direct line of firing between the Americans and Japanese lines. Many of the shells fell short of their target and landed in the camp. There were several direct hits on the buildings and many of the internees were killed. One of the shells landed just in front of our 'shanty' leaving a large crater. Luckily for me I had just left the 'shanty' for a place behind the main buildings that we used for shelter. Also during this time Manila was being bombed heavily by the planes flying overhead. I could always tell by the sound whether they were American or Japanese planes.

Our diet was now supplemented by army rations. As far as I can remember it was mostly beans. We also hung around American soldiers who were so generous in giving what they could. One soldier on seeing Stephen and me sitting outside our shanty gave us two cans of ration milk. We probably looked like two ghosts to him and he obviously felt very sorry for us.

But life went on as usual for several months more while we awaited a passage on a ship. First we went to America where we left Maude, who was American, while Stephen and I went to England. It was a joyous day to be reunited with my family after a separation of four years.''

I was unaware of the heavy fighting that had taken place while the Americans were liberating the Philippines and Santa Tomas University. Had I known it would have been extremely hard to take, it was very much a case of "ignorance is bliss" at that time.

When we sailed into Manila Bay that September day in 1945 it was a terrible sight. The bay was filled with the masts of sunken ships — there seemed hardly room to manoeuvre. Looking at the waterfront from the ship through binoculars (we were not allowed to land) it presented a very sad picture, the buildings still stood but the windows were all blown out. A few years after the war, a group of Japanese headed by Mr. Niro Hoshijima, a member of parliament, committed his government to clear the harbour as a part in making amends for what they had done to Manila during the war. Later in 1956, when I visited Manila, I was glad to see that they had kept their promise.

We were about a week anchored in Manila Bay, it was very crowded on the ship and very hot and we still had no confirmation of the date of our departure or where we were to go. We heard later that they had even considered sending us back to Hong Kong, this may have only been hearsay, but I am sure there would have been a riot if this had happened. We were of course all the time taking on more P.O.W.'s from the north.

Eventually we sailed for Singapore en route for England. We did not go into Singapore harbour, but anchored offshore and took on many more ex-P.O.W's which really made things terribly crowded, there was hardly sitting space on deck and of course no chairs to sit on — just the deck. Lady (Louis) Mountbatten was in Singapore at that time visiting the camps and came on board in her Red Cross uniform. She looked very thin and was working herself unstintingly as she always did. It meant a great deal to us all that she visited our ship.

I was worried about the journey home because as I have mentioned before I am a very bad sailor. However, I have never seen the sea so calm — right across the Indian Ocean and through the Mediterranean — it was like glass. We had schools of porpoise following us looking so graceful as they leapt out of the still blue water — it was beautiful to watch them. I was very grateful for the calm seas until we got to the Bay of Biscay, where unfortunately we met a storm and I was very sick until we got to Liverpool. It was a real miracle that so much of the trip had been in such perfect weather, as none of us were in the right state of health to have coped with long bouts of sea sickness. The real discomfort of the trip was the crowd, the noise, the boredom, and the tramp of many feet going for ever round and round the decks.

For many of us the first time on land as free men and women was when we arrived at Colombo where I hoped to meet Christopher, but by this time he was in England working at the Admiralty and was now a Commander so I had to be patient a while longer. There was a great crowd on deck after we docked, people jostling about hoping to make some long awaited contact or just out of curiosity hoping they might meet an unexpected one, as I did. I was looking around hoping to see a familiar face when suddenly I saw our old friend Jim Skinner from the Chinese Maritime Customs. He joined the navy at the same time as Christopher in Hong Kong and later had escaped (on the night of our surrender) with a group of others on a launch into China and overland to India. Several of our friends were in this group and I was reprimanded after the war for not going with them. I must admit I cannot remember ever having been asked! However, it had been a day of terrible uncertainties and I had spent most of that 24 hours smoking to try and steady my nerves and have only a hazy recollection of events; in fact, one of the men gave me a photo of a girl-friend for safe-keeping in my suitcase and after the war I returned it to the wrong man! It was the first and last time I have smoked seriously.

I was certainly overjoyed to see Jim and to find he had permission to take me ashore until we sailed early next morning. I was taken to a nice comfortable bungalow along the Gallface Road with a long narrow garden overlooking the ocean. It was so strange to sink into an easy chair again — to have my own bedroom with the usual bed in the centre to catch the breeze — to have a nice dinner brought by Jim's servant — to try and catch up with the news and happenings of the world — and in the evening to lean on the wall at the bottom of the garden looking out over the water with such glorious peace and quiet all round and try to visualize what the future might bring.

It was not easy to go back to that crowded ship, but on we went until we arrived at Suez where we went ashore to be fitted out with necessities such as clothes, shoes, a little linen bag with scissors and cotton from the Red Cross (the scissors I now use to cut bacon rind), a vest from the Lord Mayor of London, and many other welcome gifts. It was wonderful to feel remembered and we were very grateful. It was also helpful to be allowed off the ship away from the crowd and to stand on firm ground for a short spell.

Then on our way home again which was what we were all anxiously waiting for, and eventually to dock at Liverpool on a grey chilly

25th October 1945. We had at least reached our destination and poor old England just was not ready for us. They had so recently come through their own tragedies and traumas and were still weary.

In the turmoil and the crowd I suddenly saw Christopher, looking very smart in his 'brass hat' and long blue overcoat. Immediately I felt so odd in my stretched-down coat and skirt. He seemed at once so familiar and yet a stranger — so long ago since I had seen him. I remember taking his arm and we wandered stiffly through the crowd, I think both feeling very self-conscious. It was then that an 'inferiority complex' really took over — a great loneliness and the sadness of it all. We had to start all over again, almost strangers — three years and eight months is a long time — with all the unknown difficulties that lay ahead, not being able to start where we left off, war and internment saw to that, but both wanting to succeed, which was our salvation in the end. To quote a well-known politician "Life wasn't meant to be easy" . . . Very wise words and so worthwhile to battle through. When we got to the beautiful old hotel in Liverpool (but oh, so shabby then), Christopher gave me a lovely fur coat that Aunt Corrie had left me and I was very grateful to cover up some of my own shabbiness before we left by train for London.

It was a couple of days before I was able to meet Patricia and my mother, who were living in Colchester where Patricia was at school. I went to Liverpool St. Station which was packed with people waiting for trains, nobody knew what time any train would arrive or leave, one just had to wait and watch the board and hope you were meeting the right train. I was talking to a man whose wife and son had left London when the bombing started and he had no idea where to wait either, when suddenly I turned round to see the searching faces of my mother and Patricia in the crowd! Patricia had said to my mother "There's a lady over there, is that her?" and she was right. We went and had a cup of coffee in the crowded station restaurant, just to have somewhere to sit and look at each other. Patricia had brought me a jar of cold cream, an almost unobtainable gift after the war. They had to return to Colchester almost immediately, so as to get back in the day, as there was absolutely nowhere to stay in London at that time. The time-tables, chaos, and crowds were unbelievable and very confusing to me after so long locked away from the world. But I had seen them and a short time later I went to Colchester on the spur of the moment and stayed the night at their rooms. They looked so surprised when I walked in but I felt much better after my short visit to them. Later we were able to change our rooms in London to a bedsitter in West Hampstead with another room for Patricia. Christopher was still at the Admiralty and was not demobilised until well into 1946. So it was hard to get accommodation or to make plans for the future.

I had great difficulty in getting any washing done as there were no facilities in our bed-sitter, just a tiny kitchenette and a communal bathroom. One day I saw a laundry shop up the road and I took my large bundle of washing tied in a sheet. There was a determined faced lady behind the counter and several people waiting. When my turn came I asked if she could take my washing and she replied "Not unless you were registered before the war". I said "I was living in China before the war and have been a prisoner for three and a half years, so I couldn't possibly have been registered". She looked at me and said "Well, you don't look too bad!" With that I hurriedly left the shop and burst into tears. I met one of the ladies in the street who had been in the laundry at the same time and she consoled me, still holding my bundle of washing. In the end I had to send it to my sister-in-law in Oxford. It was quite impossible for any 'newcomer' to get washing done in London. A wonderful welcome home! But I guess I must have looked dishonest and she thought that I was putting a 'fast one' across. As I said, England just wasn't ready for an influx of people who really needed great care — and London was about the worst place — though it was no fault of the people. While we waited for our future plans to materialize, Patricia went daily to the well-known Francis Holland school in London.

Eventually Christopher was demobilized and we went to Wembley to collect his civilian 'entitlement' consisting of a suit, a pair of shoes, a hat, a raincoat and a shirt. Now we were on our own with no job and many difficulties ahead. Christopher had been offered his job back in the Chinese Customs, but Patricia and I would not have been allowed to return to China at that time, and after the long and unhappy separation during the war it would have been quite disastrous from a personal point of view. As it happened, the Chinese Customs did not survive after the communists took over the country — the staff was paid off in 1949. And so an unique and interesting organization came to a sad end after 90 years.

We settled down in Oxford and were fortunate enough to find a small house for sale; they were few-and-far-between at that time. We installed the furniture and house-hold things generously left me by my Aunt Marion. Such a wonderful gift for us after we had lost everything and things were in short supply and difficult to get. So we set up house with high hopes of making a home again, but the difficulties were just too varied and too great to cope with all at once, and it was not a very happy time. We were very difficult people at that time and our problems seemed insurmountable — sadly we had grown apart from each other. This made it doubly hard to cope with the problems of establishing ourselves in post-war Britain. By this time we had not lived or worked in Britain for the last twelve years, and Patricia and I were still not fit in health.

We were supposed to get one extra egg a week on our ration of one, which was not nearly enough for us. It was not until my friend Nancy Pears from Waddington sold us six hens and started us off with a bag of wheat from the farm to feed them that our health picked up dramatically. We had to give up our egg ration so that we could draw feed for the hens. The venture was a great help to us both.

The winter of 1946-7 was a very severe one and I developed pellagra (malnutrition sores) down the back of legs and heels, and at the end of the day when I got tired I had to take off any tight clothes as my body swelled up and was very uncomfortable. The swelling continued in a lessening degree for many years. I also had great difficulty in concentrating when tired — never one of my strong points! but at that time quite devastating psychologically. Thanks to the extra eggs in our diet, our health returned quicker than it would have done otherwise. It was a winter of snow, ice and burst waterpipes, and driving with chains on the car. However we joined the Caledonian Society and learnt the reels — went to the Ball and danced the 'Gay Gordons' and kept as warm as possible.

When we knew we were going to Oxford to live, I went from London to arrange for Patricia to go as a temporary boarder to "Wychwood' till we moved. It was a nice school but I had not understood how much the girls were left to work on their own and Patricia came home with many queries about her work which she should have been able to get help with at school. We then realized that she needed much more individual assistance due to the regular schooling she had missed, so we put her into St. Faith's, where she found it all easier and was able to get the extra help she needed. In spite of her chequered education she did well at school — especially with figures.

After the First World War my father had tried his hand at hotel-keeping, which was not a success, and after the Second World War we tried, with my brother, to start a kitchen appliance shop, with the same result. My father thought he had a flair for hotel-keeping, after being in command of an army depot, and Christopher felt his experience in Naval Administration would fit him for shop-keeping!

144

Salesmanship is a different thing altogether and we eventually decided farming was more to our liking even if it was hard work. So we decided to emigrate to Australia and I suppose we could now be called 'Dinkum Aussies' — after 30 years.

We arrived at Fremantle the port of Perth, Western Australia, on a Sunday morning in January 1949. There was a strike by waterside workers so the ship's crew loaded our baggage into cargo-nets. Christopher was on the wharf watching the unloading when he saw a suitcase fall out of the net into the harbour and thought "Oh, the poor people". A sailor valiantly jumped into the harbour and rescued it. Later I saw a dripping suitcase being wheeled through the customs shed and thought how terrible for the owner, then somebody asked me if I would identify some things in a suitcase and I was horrified to see laid out on the ground the 'last-minute' things we had packed before leaving Oxford! Miraculously, nothing was damaged but the display laid out resembled a jumble sale and I felt loath to own it. However I was overjoyed to see amongst the jumble a brown paper packet containing three family minatures we had re-framed in Oxford. In fear and trembling I opened the packet to find them completely undamaged — what a relief!

The first person to greet us when we arrived in Australia was a first cousin of my mother's, Norah Davies (nee Atkinson), a daughter of one of my grandmother's brothers. We had met in London many years before but she is an Australian, born and bred. She, with her husband and daughters Robin and Bronwyn, came to Fremantle to meet our ship the S.S. *Esperance Bay*. They drove us through Kings Park and over the Causeway — at that time a wooden bridge with tramway lines over the Swan River — to Kalamunda where they lived and to the Kalamunda Hotel where we stayed while we organized ourselves.

It was a wonderful thing to be met and made welcome in our new country.

There have been vast changes in Australian hotels since then. On our first morning we found it rather strange not to be given mustard in a pot for our bacon and eggs at breakfast and when we asked for some it was brought dry in a saucer. Of course it was quite tasteless until I moistened it with a little tea! Afternoon tea was non-existent and something that my mother who had accompanied us missed very much, so we bought a small spirit stove to enable her to make her own. One afternoon she came to our room in great distress, she had difficulty in putting out the stove and it had fallen into the wastepaper basket and the paper was burning merrily! We rushed into the room and flung heavy coats and anything else we could find onto the basket and fortunately the fire was out in a minute. The proprietors never knew how near they were to losing their hotel!

We had plans to live in the country of the South West. We are not country people but have spent many happy times on properties and farms in England. We love animals and thought of dairying.

At that time there was still petrol rationing and they would not allow us any extra petrol so it was impossible to do much in the way of looking at properties far from Perth. In England people from Australia were given extra petrol coupons for travelling and we had not anticipated any difficulty in Australia. So we had to confine our search to nearer Perth. We saw nothing suitable and after three months in the Kalamunda Hotel we were anxious to get settled.

One morning I saw advertised 'Gentleman's residence — with rose garden'! Perhaps 'oranges' were mentioned! This sounded as if it *must* be different to some of the places we had seen. It *did* have some roses, also a very attractive and cool patio with a fish pond, but the house was weatherboard and asbestos although adequate to move into, there was no electricity for the washing machine etc. that I had brought from England with me, and there was no telephone. If a telegram came it was left on the gatepost a quarter of a mile from the house! So we moved into our first home in Australia.

After five years we moved to a bigger property and built our own house and called it 'Brynbella' at Bindoon and settled down to grow oranges and develop a small Poll Hereford Stud.

My mother lived mostly with us for the remainder of her life. There is a brass cross to her memory on the altar of the little Anglican Church at Chidlow.

Patricia completed her education at St. Mary's School in West Perth and left to make her own life.

Most readjustments have their difficulties, the upheaval of war is traumatic — whatever the country or nationality — just speaking the same 'mother-tongue' is certainly a great help but there is much more to it than that. The 'homing' instinct is strong in humans as well as birds, the only difference is that man has no wings!

So I write from my new country and home where I have found many friends — much happiness — and many interesting and new experiences.

Some ten years after the war had ended I received £46 reparation money from the British Government. This was money from the proceeds of the sale of Japanese assets seized by the British Government

146

at the outbreak of war with Japan. Not a very large sum when one takes into account the total loss of one's complete home and personal possessions. But personal possessions are not everything. We had come out of it with our lives and a future to build however hard it might be.

I have written my story in gratitude for kindnesses given, shared, and remembered in times of great peace or great adversity, by those of different nationalities and backgrounds. I hope my friends old and new in both hemispheres find something of interest in my story which spans some seventy years. Many places and people are in this book and many more will be in my memory forever, growing closer as the years progress.

'Oh time — turn back — and give me just one hour
upon the China soil where I was born'

from a book by Dorothy Loosley

The author L. with Mrs. Nell Labrousse in Sydney 1979. (Nell Hale)

H.M.S. SCOUT. Hong Kong Local Defence Flotilla.

APPENDIX I

H.M.S. 'SCOUT'

The story would not be complete without the tale of *H.M.S. Scout* after December, 1941. It was not until October 1945 that Christopher was able to tell me the rest of the story. Gladly would I have sailed away in her too — had I had the chance to do so.

H.M.S. Scout was built in 1918 and was believed to have fired a shot in anger in the North Sea area before the end of the Great War. She was one of three of a class stationed in Hong Kong as a local Defence Flotilla. The other two were *Thracian* and *Thanet*. The morning of Monday 8th December 1941, found *Scout* lying in the dry-dock at Taikoo shipyard having her bottom cleaned and painted. Fortunately this had just been completed and the ship was ready to be refloated.

It was about 7 a.m. when Christopher phoned me to say that we were at war with Japan and while he was talking the first air raid took place, and as I have mentioned before, they attacked Kai Tak where the Pan-Am flying boat was destroyed. Christopher hastily put down the receiver and the ship went to Air Attack Stations. By this time *Scout* was raising steam and needed to get the dry-dock flooded. However, the Chinese workmen for the dry-dock had failed to turn up so there was some delay until European dock staff could be summoned to show the ship's crew how to flood the dock. Eventually the dock was flooded and Christopher says a real sigh of relief went up when the ship was safely out in the harbour.

At lunchtime that day we met for a few minutes, as arranged, at the dockyard gate and I handed over a basket with a few clothes. Little did I know it was to be the last meeting for over three and a half years. That afternoon Christopher's captain Lt. Commander Hedworth Lambton R.N. sent for him and made him promise that he would not get in touch with me but he would arrange for a letter to be delivered to me through the S.O.O. (Staff Officer Operations), and he then told Christopher that *Scout* and *Thanet* were to proceed to Singapore that night and to get the ship ready for sea.

Scout passed through the boom outside Lyemun Pass at 9 p.m. following *Thanet* who was senior ship, and the next port was to be Manila. Two passengers were taken aboard who had come from Chungking and were considered important enough to be given passage out of the Colony. One was Colin MacDonald, a correspondent for The Times, and the other was a Mr. Wint, who was from the British Embassy in Chungking. The ships arrived in Manila late afternoon on 10th December. During the time they were nearing Manila they received signals direct from the *Prince of Wales* and *Repulse* off Singapore giving details of the action with Japanese aircraft. Sadly by the time they reached Manila these two great ships had been sunk — a tragic setback in the early stages of the war with Japan.

While fueling in Manila Christopher's cousin Stephen Crawfurd came to the ship to see him. Patricia was at this time up at Baguio with Maude Crawfurd so he had to proceed on his way without seeing her. If I had been able to smuggle myself on board *Scout* I would have been put ashore at Manila and would, at least, have been with Patricia for the duration of the war, but this was not to be.

The two ships arrived in Singapore having called at Tarakan and Batavia (as it was then) for fuel. Here they separated and *Scout* was sent to patrol in the Malacca Straits — *Thanet* to other duties. The latter was sunk by the Japanese cruiser when she went to intercept the first of the landings on the east coast of Malaysia. *Scout* finally left Singapore on the 10th February 1942 and fortunately had an uneventful run to Batavia — the weather was cloudy during the passage and it was probably due to this that they were not spotted by Japanese aircraft.

Passengers were embarked before leaving Singapore, mainly naval ratings, most of whom were survivors from the *Prince of Wales* and *Repulse*. Also embarked was Mrs. Megan Spooner, wife of Rear Admiral Spooner, who lost his life while escaping from Singapore. Mrs. Spooner was better known as 'Megan Foster' the concert singer. Among others embarking were the Admiral's staff consisting of the Flag Lieutenant, Coxswain, and Steward, and the whole party arrived safely at Batavia and were put on board the *S.S. City of Bedford* for passage to Australia.

It was busy days for *Scout*. After the fall of Singapore, the whole area became crowded with shipping and people doing their best to escape from the victorious Japanese advance and it was soon realized that Java was not going to last long. The harassment by the Japanese aircraft was constant — coupled with probing forays of Japanese surface craft and submarines — all of which took their toll of our forces.

Scout, together with *Tennedos* — a destroyer of the same class that had been based at Singapore — joined the 'screen' of three cruisers — *HMAS Hobart, HMS's Dragon* and *Danae* — who were escorting merchant ships west through the Sunda Straits to the comparative safety of the Indian Ocean. When the last days of Java were in sight this small escort force was ordered to Colombo. On the way there they stopped off at the small port of Padang on the west coast of Sumatra, and it was here that some 2,000 people had collected, mainly civilian and of diverse nationalities who had escaped from Singapore. The two destroyers proceeded to ferry these people out to the cruisers — *Tennedos* making two trips and *Scout* one, taking some 600 people each trip. Anyone arriving at Padang after that night was subsequently captured by the Japanese.

On arrival in Colombo this force was dispersed and *Scout* joined the destroyers of Admiral Somerville's Eastern fleet in the Indian Ocean. This consisted of *Warspite* and a number of old battleships with attendant cruisers and destroyers. *Tennedos* was by now suffering from engine and boiler trouble and was subsequently damaged in an air raid over Colombo harbour. After some weeks of cruising this fleet was ordered to proceed to Killindini, in East Africa.

Unfortunately for *Scout*, her fuel range was not long enough for the trip and she was left behind at Colombo. She paid-off there and the ship's company were returned to Britain, except Christopher, who was posted for duty to Bombay.

While in Colombo a visitor came on board to see Christopher, namely John Douglas, who I have mentioned earlier, and who was able to tell Christopher that he had seen me at Aberdeen and at least I was alive at the surrender of Hong Kong. This was the first news he had had of me since he left Hong Kong and it was now early May 1942.

APPENDIX II

LINKS WITH THE PAST

General Sir Henry Beresford Willcox. K.C.I.E., C.B., D.S.O., M.C.

To find in Western Australia a man who joined my father's regiment (the 2nd Battalion Sherwood Foresters) when he was twenty-one and I was eight was an unexpected and pleasurable surprise. That man was Beresford Willcox. He was born and brought up in New Zealand and served his military career with the British Army. He joined the Battalion when it was stationed at Crown Hill near Plymouth in about 1912 and that was where I first met him when he came to 'call' on my parents. My father retired soon after that and they lost touch.

I had been told the story of how the 2nd Battalion was wiped out in France — all but one officer and 27 men — and how that might have been my father's fate had he gone to France instead of Gallipoli with another battalion. I never knew who the officer was until we went to stay with the Willcox's in Bridgetown, Western Ausralia and while reminiscing he told me *he* was that officer. What a long way to travel before finding that out! Beresford was a gallant and popular man with great charm and dignity. Some of his war-time relics can be seen in the W.A. Army Museum in Perth and are most interesting.

Captain Wan

While we were in Chefoo in 1936-37 Christopher had a Chinese 2nd Officer on the Custom Cruiser *Huahsing* named Wan Tong Chu — now Captain Wan of Perth, W.A. Before joining the ship he had married one of the well-known Fong family from Geraldton, W.A. She could only speak 'Australian' and the ship's crew were puzzled at this Chinese lady who could not speak Chinese! They have a daughter and son, Shirley and Brian. Shirley was born in Chefoo when we were there.

After a lapse of many years we were delighted to meet them all again in Perth. Shirley married Rahman Yahaya from Malaysia and we were privileged to be at their wedding reception. Brian married Blossom Tan from Singapore. Both have families and we meet from time to time.

Mr. Colin MacDonald

Soon after we arrived in Australia we heard a radio broadcast from the man who had escaped from Hong Kong in *H.M.S. Scout*. That man was Mr. Colin MacDonald who had returned to his home State to live. It appears now that he only went to Hong Kong to file messages for his paper the 'London Times' as it was difficult to do so from Chungking, the war-time capital of China, owing to the Chinese censorship. The sudden attack by the Japanese took him by surprise and he was unable to return direct to Chungking. Fortunately for him *H.M.S Scout* was leaving Hong Kong and took him as far as Tarakan, Borneo. He eventually returned to Chungking via Singapore and Rangoon.

Since that broadcast we have had some happy meetings with Colin MacDonald in Perth, W.A.

A Japanese Luncheon

Another interesting experience we had was a lunch party we gave on our citrus farm at Bindoon, W.A. in 1965. We invited a group of nine young Japanese business men, led by 70-year-old Mr. Soji Fuji, who had come on a trade trip. I chose the menu carefully and as a centre-piece on the table I arranged a square glass dish of mock-orange flowers with a red rose in the centre, depicting the Japanese flag. This created great interest and was duly photographed. Mr. Soji Fuji understood English quite well but was unable to speak much; however, one of the party was American-educated so we were able to converse. During lunch it came out that I had been a prisoner of their country during the war. There was a hush round the table and then Mr. Soji Fuji said to me "I am very sorry for all the suffering you have had" and I felt he really meant what he said. It turned out that also at the table was a young Japanese who had spent nine years as a prisoner of the Russians in Manchuria. It was an interesting lunch and I was glad to have had the opporunity of receiving those young Japanese men in my home.

A Visit to America

After our migration to Australia we visited America and at a lunch party I met an American Japanese who had been interned in America during the war. He was telling those present of the hardships he suffered in an internment camp and the meagre rations of "only a tin of this or that". He did not know at the time that I had been a prisoner under Japanese rule.

I listened to what he had to say and after lunch told him of some of my own experiences — the poor man looked shattered! He apologized to me most humbly. I would have thought myself lucky to have had one of his 'tins'.

Mr. P.O. (Paddy) Bowers of Busselton, W.A.

Another 'link with the past' came one evening at a Returned Servicemen's party at Busselton. Somebody introduced me to Paddy Bowers and told him that I had been a prisoner at Stanley Camp in Hong Kong. Mr. Bowers was most interested and told me how his ship *H.M.A.S. Cairns* had been the first ship to enter the harbour after the Japanese had surrendered. *H.M.A.S. Cairns* was a minesweeper attached to Admiral Harcourt's relieving force, and Paddy was Stoker Petty Officer on that ship. He described how they swept the harbour for mines and then 'showed-the-flag' in the many inlets of Hong Kong harbour in order to let the people know that the Japanese had gone at last.

One of the things that most impressed Paddy about lying in Hong Kong harbour was the 'side-party' system. Before the war all H.M. ships in Hong Kong would have a Chinese family with their 'sampan' attached to the ship. A sampan is a boat of smallish size propelled by a single oar at the stern, or sail, and a bamboo canopy under which a family can live, spending their entire lives. Their duty was to keep the ship's side clean and touch up the paint when needed. In return they collected the food refuse, some of this they used themselves and the remainder would be sold. The sampan could be used as a ferry to the shore or to carry messages. *Cairns* had no sooner anchored in the harbour than a 'side-party' attached themselves to her. The family consisted of a man and his wife and a little girl who were in a bad way, having suffered from food shortages during the Japanese occupation and they were put on full rations as well as getting the refuse. Paddy gave the little girl her 'first ever' piece of chocolate and remembers her delight as she eventually plucked up courage to taste it. Each time *Cairns* returned to harbour their 'side-party' was there to greet them.

Paddy was in *H.M.A.S. Hobart* at the time of the fall of Singapore and remembers *H.M.S. Scout* and *Tennedos* ferrying people out to his ship who had escaped from Singapore to Padang, a small port on the west coast of Sumatra. Paddy was with *Hobart* until she was damaged by a torpedo in the Pacific and he was injured.

Mr. Alf Binks

A very remarkable meeting took place in Perth when Christopher and I attended a Returned Services League Poppy Day Dinner given in 1979 during the Sesqui-Centennial celebrations of the State of Western Australia. There we were introduced to Mr. and Mrs. Binks (Alf and Yolande) and discovered our close connections with pre-war China and how our paths had so nearly met in Chefoo.

I have since heard from Alf how his father and mother (China Inland Missionaries from Yunnan in S. W. China) were briefly in Stanley Camp when I was there but we never met. They were caught while on their way to visit their family of four children in Chefoo for the first time in six years and to take them to Australia on furlough, so yet another plan never eventuated due to war.

Alf Binks' story is both fascinating and interesting and one that I have not seen referred to anywhere else and only came to my knowledge by a fortuitous meeting nearly forty years after the war.

Alf Binks was born and brought up in Akumi, a small tribal village nestling on the slopes on the China side of the Himalayas above the Salween River in the province of Yunnan. His mother tongue was Lisu, spoken by his parents in their dealings with the tribal people. His most vivid recollections of those days was a raid on the village by a band of Chinese brigands. Hiding in their home they could hear the cries of the village folk as the bandits went from house to house on a spree of pillage and carnage.

At the age of five Alf and his twin brother and two sisters were sent to boarding school over a thousand miles away to the well-known China Inland Mission School at Chefoo in Shantung, N.E. China, where we had been stationed. (*Pigtails, Petticoats, and The Old School Tie*' by Sheila Miller, gives the history of the original Chefoo School that now operates in many lands other than China.)

Under the school system, the Binks' were due to see their parents at least every two years; however, being so far away and because of the intervention of events due to the Japanese invasion of China in 1937 leading up to the entry of Japan into the war with the bombing of Pearl Harbour, the family was separated for six years.

After Pearl Harbour Japanese soon appropriated the school properties for military headquarters and the children and staff were evicted and marched through the town, carrying their belongings, to three large foreign residences where they were interned and forced to improvise a way of life with inadequate accommodation. Under these conditions the process of education resumed in a limited fashion.

After eleven months the Japanese decided to transfer about 300 children and staff in a troopship, the *'Kioda Maru'*, to a Presbyterian Mission College further south at Weishien. The conditions on the ship were harsh, and for two days and nights seasick children were housed in lower open decks on straw mats infested with cockroaches and rats. On arrival at Tsingtao, all were crammed into a troop train, tired and hungry, for the journey inland to Weishien, where 2,000 occupants of the camp gaped in surprise at this new group of internees sent to join them. In such a large camp the life was hard and they had to line up for hours for meals, washrooms etc. The school had great difficulty in keeping adequate control of the children and some undesirable associations developed. Alf joined up with a small gang engaged in smuggling stovepipes from the Japanese storage buildings. The winter was bitterly cold and the internees built stoves in their huts for warmth, hence the market for stovepipes. These were exchanged by the gang for food, chocolates, chewing gum, etc. Unfortunately they were caught in the act by the Japanese and being minors were handed over to the camp leaders for punishment. Loss of privileges and the disgrace which followed left an indelible mark on his life and he has never stolen stovepipes again!

In about 18 months a rumour spread that about 40 children were to be taken south to Shanghai. The school was assembled and the names of the children called out, among the names were four 'Pink' children but none answered that description — eventually it was determinded that it was the 'Binks' children who had been nominated! The Swiss Red Cross had secured agreement with the Japanese for children separated from their parents for many years to be reunited in a camp at Chapei in Shanghai.

The trip from Weishien to Shanghai was an incredible experience for 40 children accompanied by a Swiss official and travelling in a Japanese troop train. They sat for hours in crowded carriages with all the shutters down for blackout purposes and the foul smell of the vile tobacco smoked by the Japanese soldiers. It was too much for Alf and eventually he was violently sick and the guard sitting next to him became the recipient, much to his disgust!

Alf found that being united with his parents after seven years from the age of five was a strange and disturbing experience. However, before long these strangers won his love and they took up a form of family life in Chapei. Each family was allocated an area of floor space according to their number and as there were six in their group they were fortunate to get a window. Each family was separated by only a curtain, so peace, quiet, and privacy was almost unknown as one can imagine with a dozen families living in the one area 24 hours a day.

In 1945 frequent air raids over Shanghai from allied carrier-based planes forshadowed the end of hostilities and finally the Swiss authorities announced VJ day and the Japanese guards fled, leaving the internees to be repatriated to their homelands. So freedom came for Alf Binks at the age of 13 after 3½ years of internment.

Because his father was Australian, they were repatriated on the hospital ship *H.M.S. 'Gerusalemme'* to Fremantle, continuing their journey by *H.M.A.S. 'Berwick'* to Sydney in time to spend Christmas on their grandfather's farm in New South Wales after eight year's absence.

During a holiday in Perth some years later Alf decided to settle there and met and married his wife Yolande. Through that chance meeting in 1979 we realize how closely our paths ran together without quite meeting.

Alf also found he had 'links-with-the-past' in Perth through a microbiologist named Stewart Goodwin. They were at the Chefoo school together and went through the same war-time experiences. Stewart married the daughter of one of the headmasters and has also settled in Perth.

Mr. Archie Fontanini M.B.E.

A well-known personality in Western Australia was Mr. Archie Fontanini who lived near Manjimup in the south-west. He settled in the area in 1907 and constructed a pool to 'spell' the soil from over-cropping with potatoes. This was to become known as 'Fonty's Pool' and for many years it was a popular waterhole for the district. Later he landscaped the area and staged woodchopping competitions and other attractions.

Mr. Fontanini was awarded the M.B.E. in 1970 for services to the Manjimup district. In 1972 he received the gold medal of the Italian Chamber of Commerce. On 14th 1980, Mr. Fontanini celebrated his 100th birthday which will be remembered by an engraved plaque in the foothpath of the Manjimup Shire Office to mark his life and work.

One day we were motoring in the district and decided to go and see the 'Pool'. We were fortunate enough to meet Mr. Fontanini and while talking to him I discovered that as a lad he was in the Italian Army and was part of the Italian Legation Guard in Peking when I was born there in 1903.

This meeting seems truly a part of my long journey from 'PEKING TO PERTH' as Manjimup is not very far south of Perth, W.A.

ARTLOOK BOOKS

PATHWAYS TO INDEPENDENCE
Dame Rachel Cleland, pp.

Memories of Papua/New Guinea of which her husband Sir Donald Cleland was Administrator in the fifties. A politically important history of the emergence of the will to achieve independance by a near neighbour. Dame Rachel maintains close relationships with Papuan friends and the book is beautifully illustrated by one of the country's young artists.

THE GINGKO TREE
Rix Weaver, 270 pp.

A novel on the grand scale. Diana Ashton, of Italian descent, is the fourth generation to have lived in the magnificent station homestead in New South Wales. She is a lovable person drawn convincingly on a canvas that also depicts her parents, her husband and her four children. Mrs. Weaver is a practising Jungian analyist and the author of a number of best selling books.

MY COUNTRY
C. K., 96 pp.

A history of Vietnam, simply told in English/Vietnamese captions to detailed black and white drawings. The author is a young student now living in Australia and the book is invaluable for anyone who wants to study the background or language of the Vietnamese.

CULT COUNTER CULT
Lloyd Davies, pp.

A novel on the brainwashing techniques of a religious commune and the equally obnoxious practises of a hired "de-programmer". Good plot, cleverly told, bawdily humorous in parts. The author, a practising solicitor, makes use of his knowledge in the sequences dealing with legal matters. This is his second book.

THE HAPPY CHILDREN
Joseph Raffa, pp.

A nostalgic account of the lives of the Italian fishing community in Fremantle before World War II. A simple and delightful tale, with photographs. English/Italian edition.

CASEY'S WIFE

Dorothy Congden-Casey, 296 pp, $11.95 h.c.

Author/Journalist Gavin Casey is portrayed with compassion and insight in this autobiography of his first wife. The account of her childhood and youth on the Goldfields is a historically valuable bonus.

THE LEGEND OF SAM CHALWELL

Norm Fuller, 108 pp.

Journalists account of Sam Chalwells hunt for treasure which, he believed until his death in 1965, was buried on his Rockingham farm. A fascinating mystery, still unsolved.

NO BORROWED GOLD

Alec Phillips, 164 pp.

Unique account of early survey excursions along the border of Western Australia and the Northern Territory and development of a farming property at Kojonup. Remarkable for its collection of photographs taken on the survey camps.

CATS DOGGEREL

Joan Brodsgaard, 80pp.

There has never been a book like this, a collection of narrative verse written by the **cats themselves** (aided by Joan Brodsgaard, who also sketched the authors). Rugged types like Harry Battler and the sleek, sophisticated siamese sirens. Printed on fine quality paper with black and white illustrations. A delightful gift for any cat lover.

THE GREAT RIDE

Henry Bostock, 236 pp.

Helped by notes and a diary kept at the time, Henry Bostock in his eighty-seventh year, wrote a very readable and most valuable account of that epic ride which immortalised the 10th Light Horse. Includes numerous photos taken in the field. A must for historians and collectors of military literature.

SOUVENIR

By Hal Colebatch, 123 pp.

The lunatic side to literature is explored in this new Australian novel. A Writing Bee on an island sets the scene for an uproarious literary Gotterdaemmerung.